Praise for Don't Kill the Bosses!

"*Don't Kill the Bosses!* offers a valuable new approach to management philosophy. It makes one rethink traditional boss/employee relationships."

> —Glenda Grant, President, Hearst Entertainment

"When issuing directives and asserting myself I've always tried to think about the other person's knowledge and experience. This book has provided additional sensitivity—most essentially, the importance of hiring people who know more than you and the structure that allows them to excel."

> —Paul Koplin, President, Venture Technologies Group, LLC

"*Don't Kill the Bosses!* reveals a practical, sensible and inherently intuitive paradigm for the management of hierarchical relationships. It's an easy read, well salted with real-life case studies, communicating a clear message to anyone who reports to someone or has someone reporting to them."

> —Gordon W. Perkin, M.D., Director, Global Health Program,
> Bill and Melinda Gates Foundation

"You will learn in this book that two-sided accountability leads to straight talk and better communications. Finally, a book with practical advice that managers can use day-to-day to get better results."

> —Philip J. Harkins, President and CEO, Linkage Inc.

"What the authors call 'the obvious' is a refreshing awareness of dealing with relationships both inside and outside the workplace. Two-sided accountability is the foundation for any successful organization, however, until now, there never has been such an insightful review of the concept. In short, this is an unforgettable book."

> —Donald L. Struminger, Chairman of the Board,
> Virginia Linen Service

Don't Kill
the Bosses!

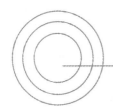

Don't Kill the Bosses!

Escaping the Hierarchy Trap

Samuel A. Culbert

John B. Ullmen

BK

BERRETT-KOEHLER PUBLISHERS, INC.
San Francisco

Berrett-Koehler Publishers, Inc.
235 Montgomery Street, Suite 650
San Francisco, CA 94104-2916
Tel: (415) 288-0260
Fax: (415) 362-2512
www.bkconnection.com

ORDERING INFORMATION
Quantity sales. Special discounts are available on quantity purchases by corporations, associations, and others. For details, contact the "Special Sales Department" at the Berrett-Koehler address above.

Individual sales. Berrett-Koehler publications are available through most bookstores. They can also be ordered direct from Berrett-Koehler: Tel: (800) 929-2929; Fax: (802) 864-7626; www.bkconnection.com

Orders for college textbook/course adoption use. Please contact Berrett-Koehler:Tel: (800) 929-2929; Fax: (802) 864-7626.

Orders by U.S. trade bookstores and wholesalers. Please contact Publishers Group West, 1700 Fourth Street, Berkeley, CA 94710. Tel: (510) 528-1444; Fax (510) 528-3444.

Production Management. Michael Bass & Associates

Printed in the United States of America
Printed on acid-free and recycled paper that is composed of 85% recovered fiber, including 15% post consumer waste.

Library of Congress Cataloging-in-Publication Data

Culbert, Samuel A.
    Don't kill the bosses : escaping the hierarchy trap / by Samuel A. Culbert and John B. Ullmen.
    p. cm.
    Includes bibliographical references and index.
    ISBN 1-57675-161-9
    1. Organizational change. 2. Corporate culture. 3. Supervisors. I. Ullmen, John B., 1966- II. Title.

HD58.8 .C85 2001
650.1'3—dc21   2001025542

First Edition
  05   04   03   02   01   10 9 8 7 6 5 4 3 2 1

Rosella

Contents

Preface

When it comes to thinking about difficult situations you face at work, interactions between you and your boss or between you and your direct reports probably rank amongst the most challenging. If you're like most of us, any difficulty can seem like *Friday the 13th* and *Nightmare on Elm Street* rolled up into one long movie that goes on and on without ending. We know about this because we're in the business of helping people solve the work situations they find most troubling. Even bosses who complacently reason that the absence of smoke means "no fire" eventually discover what this apparent serenity has cost their company. And in almost every instance, their subordinates knew well in advance about the problem but felt at peril to send out so much as a single smoke signal.

Had we done a double-blind study, we couldn't be more convinced of our belief that boss/subordinate relationships constitute the number one selling agent for tranquilizers, antacids, and beta-blockers and probably account for more people losing their jobs than market downturns and personal incompetence. Even people who don't have a problem today will tell you about a terrible relationship they had with a boss or subordinate in the past. They will candidly admit to not feeling out of the woods when it comes to thinking about tomorrow. And we're not just talking about bosses and subordinates; we're talking about all unequal power relationships such as those between buyers and suppliers and big and small company joint ventures and partnerships. In today's work world, few know how to deal fairly and constructively with a hierarchical relationship in which one party feels entitled to dominate. This kind of relationship poses a continuing threat to your everyday effectiveness and productivity. Like most people, you probably know of few solutions other than fault-finding divorce and resource-defeating breakup. This book gives you a new and far more constructive remedy.

We propose a scheme for humanizing boss/subordinate relationships. We want to make it possible for you to get the troubling issues out on the table where they can be forthrightly engaged. It's a scheme that cuts to the heart of what's wrong in even the most successfully run organizations and companies. We dislike the "subordinate" treatment that most people receive from their boss, but no more than we dislike the "superior" treatment most bosses receive from the people reporting to them, as bosses and subordinates alike confuse such operational basics as responsibility, authority, and accountability. We know there's confusion; otherwise, boss-dominated relationships would not be the default setting behind most managerial interactions.

Boss-dominated relationships! What a strange and nonsensical state of affairs. After all that's been said about the advantages of empowerment, participatory decision making, and team play, how is it possible that we continue allowing bosses to dominate and subordinates to fake acquiescence to the extent that both do today? It's a particularly ludicrous situation when you consider the proliferation of new organization effectiveness models put forth in contemporary management books. In fact every effectiveness scheme we've seen prescribes straightforward boss/subordinate communications, the type that inspires mutual confidence. Some go so far as to propose Sunday school lists for achieving honest, give-and-take interactions that have created more book sales than real-time improvements. None alludes to positives in getting subordinates to knuckle under, view situations as the boss sees them, and generally to do what they are told—conditions rife in today's workplace.

It's a situation we've been analyzing for years, looking for a strategic way of changing things. Finally we uncovered the obvious. It's an idea that will seem so everyday familiar that at first you might think we're merely attaching conceptual handles to what you were on the brink of realizing based on your own experience. But understanding alone will not lead you to a better course of action. To make self-meaningful and organization effectiveness changes, you need to do something more. You need to reconcile the "disconnect" between what you know about human nature and other people, and the illogic that underlies how you actually behave when acting as boss or subordinate or alternating between both. Until you reconcile this disconnect, it'll be boss domination/subordinate submission as usual, with the virtues of hierarchy unrealized.

We hope you find the *Don't Kill the Bosses!* perspective personally clarifying and a resource in making your entire company more effective. Minimally it should provide you a more accurate picture of the teamwork difficulties you've experienced and precisely what about your work relationships needs changing. Maximally it can infuse hierarchical relationships with a real measure of accountability to invigorate and reify team play. Of course, specific uses you make will depend on your role, gutsiness, and the situation.

Samuel Culbert, Santa Monica, California
John Ullmen, Los Angeles, California
June 2001

Acknowledgments

Two problems occur when acknowledging people who help with a book. The first pertains to the fact that a book is a work by many for which only one or two get the credit. The second relates to the fact that, in our case, allotting credit based on percentage of contribution would net the authors but ten bucks in royalties.

So, at the risk of leaving ourselves no credit, we want to thank people whose efforts made this book worthwhile. First, foremost, and grandest is Carolee Howell who, for the second time, showed herself to be the most tasteful and responsive editor any writer could hope to find.

Next is our arch supporter Warren Bennis. Talk about your giants! He's ours. All of his friends know that Warren is enormously generous with his time. We know that generosity also extends to his commitment, intelligence, and human concern.

Speaking of organizational heroes and the people you learn from by watching them act, Mark Shahriary is an educational prize. We've been privileged to watch him run three companies, over a time span of almost ten years, in ways that have taught us a great deal about leadership, teamwork, and hierarchy.

We had magnificent "readers," people who reviewed preliminary draft manuscripts and gave us honest commentary. All deserve star billing. In alphabetical order they are Brian Bennett, Gar Culbert, Stan Holditch, Carl Kravetz, Paul Koplin, Scott Schroeder, and Bob Tannenbaum.

Then there are the cheerleaders. Thank God for them. It gets lonely trying to fix a dangling participle at three in the morning. Notwithstanding the fact that here we could list all of our family and each friend, we'd like to mention some special people whose support was especially meaningful: Joe Alerhand, Stephanie Kagimoto, Ilene Kahn, Mel Lancet, Linda Ross, Ron and Alexandra Seigel, Jeevan Sivasubramaniam, and Rosella Forte.

Finally, our publisher Steve Piersanti deserves our special gratitude. He gets our Hot Pastrami Award for a relentless good taste that sometimes sparks indigestion. For our money he's a boss who personifies telling it straight and an individual with instincts that merit our highest praise.

Introduction and Executive Summary
Why Not Kill the Bosses?!

I don't want any "yes-men" around me. I want everybody to tell me the truth even if it costs them their jobs.

Sam Goldwyn

You don't have to read beyond Sam Goldwyn's words to see what ***Don't Kill the Bosses!*** is about. It's certainly not about killing bosses per se; it's about fixing companies by killing the reality-resistant idea of boss-dominated relationships so the virtues of hierarchy can be fully enjoyed. Operational effectiveness depends on people speaking their minds candidly, without fear that speaking the truth, as they know it, will cost them their job, pay, assignment, or career. Why would a decision maker *not* want to hear the truth from whomever was speaking it if, at the end of the day, that person knew the decision was his or hers to make and that he or she would actually be held accountable for its results? It's a situation that defies rational logic. Yet it takes place almost all the time, every day at work.

The illogic of this dynamic offers a clue to the fix required. Bosses who want to hear the truth need to create the circumstances for subordinates to tell it to them straight. Another clue comes from noting the illogic of thinking that bosses or subordinates can ever be counted on to provide a version that's totally objective. Despite the pretense of rationality, what is said and done at work is more subjective and self-interested than objective and exclusively company focused. People are self-interested; their self-interests are different than yours; and the only way to identify someone's motives and self-interests—to determine how they align with company needs and what adjustments might improve that alignment—is to inquire about them, listening carefully to what you don't hear as well as what you do.

But there's an intermediary set of interests distorting all alignments. Standing between each individual's relationship with the company is that individual's relationship with the "the boss," the person whose behavior he or she sees determining benefits and insecurities. Herein lies the perversion. Incorrectly, people place pleasing the boss above doing what's right for the company. It's a paradox. Though hierarchy provides a basic orientation and defines accountability, it also perverts relationships and ultimately damages both individual and organizational effectiveness.

On the surface most bosses ignore, and even deny, hierarchical domination, treating it as if it were a secret, business profitability expedient. If it's a secret then it's an open secret that subordinates readily discuss. They grouse about it at lunch, they complain about it in the corridors, and they seldom go in a group for an after-work drink without raising it as a topic of disdain. Every once in a while an extreme situation is sensationalized in the press like reports of intimidation and moral corruption wrecked on Sunbeam's managers when "Chainsaw" Al Dunlap was CEO. Intellectually it's a background topic in all the management and leadership books, especially those focused on participation and effective teamwork. Nevertheless, despite all the notoriety and theoretical arguments to abate it, boss domination is a relentless dynamic that doesn't go away. Bosses shamelessly exercise their "right" to dominate while subordinates manipulatively submit, putting a self-interested spin on all upwardly directed communications.

Of course, almost every boss is also a subordinate with first-hand knowledge of the double-think and truth slanting that goes into conversations with uppers. But a type of schizophrenia sets in that shields these "sometimes subordinates" from thinking that the sincere accounts their subordinates give might be infused with a devious or a self-interested spin. In fact, almost everyone, boss or subordinate, speaks as if his or her thoughts are objective and thinks likewise about the thoughts of those who agree. Spin, bias, and self-interested motives only become active suspects after disagreement is sensed.

We've done the fieldwork, analyzed the structure, and figured out what causes people to form boss-dominating relationships in which subordinates feel they better tell it the way the boss wants to hear it, depriving bosses of the version that will do them and the company the most good. What's more we know what needs to be fixed and we're ready to tell you how to produce better outcomes. But most people won't have an easy time changing. That's because what's off can't be fixed using the conventional hierarchical paradigm. Basic assumptions about people and the politics of team play need to be changed. The paradigm needs transforming.

Don't Kill the Bosses! is aimed at having transformational impact for people who are willing to spend the time in an honest, self-reflecting, cover-to-cover read. Getting these ideas into your emotions, so that your understanding of them actually influences your behavior, requires vicarious, personal learning. That's what we're hoping you'll accomplish relating to the true-life cases, stories, and dilemmas interspersed throughout this book. Each was selected for its ability to stimulate reflection about like situations that you have experienced in your own life at work. We invite you to rerun "the tapes," apply our analysis to how you felt and reasoned when you were in those situations dissatisfied, and decide for yourself whether our recommended ways of proceeding would have gotten you and your company more desirable results.

Chapter 1 begins with a broad-ranging discussion of hierarchy to help you differentiate between the positives of hierarchical structure and the negatives of hierarchical relationships. It's a distinction that most people haven't thought through sufficiently well to realize why it is so critical to make. We call not distinguishing between hierarchical structure and hierarchical relationships **the**

hierarchy trap and immediately roll out five categories of negative consequences that predictably follow: *warped communication, corrupt internal politics, illusionary teamwork, personal dispiriting,* and *pass-the-buck accountability.*

Simply put, hierarchical **structure** is the organizational chain-of-command. It's the road map for seeing who is responsible for taking what action, who has the authority to make decisions and direct, and who is supposed to oversee and insist on corrective actions when specified results are not forthcoming. Its essentiality to effective organization is without question.

In contrast, hierarchical **relationships** are the top-down, power-deferential ways people think, talk, and behave with one another when hierarchical, chain-of-command authorities are imported into problem-solving discussions. By hierarchical *relationships*, we're talking most centrally about boss/subordinate interactions, but we're talking about other nonparity relationships as well. We're also talking about relationships contracting firms have with their suppliers, relationships between joint venture partners with unequal resources, and relationships firms have with independent contractors such as specialty lawyers, auditors, consultants, and even travel agents. In every instance, when a relationship is engaged hierarchically, the company loses out. Thus, hierarchical thinking poses a burning ember threat to any business's bottom line.

Hierarchical relationships cause higher-ups to self-inflate on rank and stature, believing that they know more than they do and that people lower down the chain know less than they do. They have some basis for thinking this way because lower-downs are hesitant to speak their minds, fearing that speaking with candor will negatively affect their reviews. Instead, they see agreeing with uppers and ego-flattering as paths to outcomes they desire. We explain how such relationships stifle open-minded thinking, discussion, and cooperation and inevitably compromise corporate effectiveness.

Briefly describing the antidote to hierarchical relationships, and labeling it **"two-sided accountability,"** we present three compelling case stories chosen to illustrate the prevalence of hierarchical *relationships* and the aforementioned categories of negatives. The inner dynamics of these stories are universal to the point that we expect readers to reflect on like entrapments that they have faced without, at the time, seeing they had an alternative.

The first case depicts a classic hierarchical trap. It describes a group of managers enmeshed in hierarchical relationships trying to solve a critical lack-of-teamwork problem using the logic of command-and-control. Graphically it illustrates how hierarchical relationships preclude the very teamwork a company's management desires most. The second case shows how readily hierarchical relationships lead to warped communication, corruption, and the type of internal politics that devastates careers. The third displays the core dishonesty that shadows all hierarchical relationships, with dispiriting and self-delusion the predictable consequences. Taken together these cases begin our mapping of the destructive dynamics that inevitably accompany hierarchical relationships and serve to establish the need for what we later propose as the ultimate system remedy.

Chapter 2 first explains how the five categories—warped communication, corrupt internal politics, illusionary teamwork, personal dispiriting, and pass-the-buck accountability—overlap, each one feeding the others. Then it presents a case illustrating major problems caused by pass-the-buck accountability in the management of the LAPD. This example sets the stage for our analysis of precisely what causes hierarchical relationships to corrupt. It also allows us to establish the inevitability of the corruption, the illogic involved, and the organization ineffectiveness that results. Our focus is on interlocking dynamics, not malevolently intentioned people. The subtext bears on the dynamics created when lowers are put in self-interested binds by self-intoxicated uppers defending inflated personas.

Our analysis takes up the pay, assignment, and career progression stakes that cause subordinates to package, shade, and spin the truth to please the boss and the insecurities, ego problems, and self-inflation issues that cause bosses to take at face value what they are told. Then the discussion deepens by pinpointing precisely what causes hierarchical relationships to corrupt.

One-sided accountability! That's the cause of the problem and a relationship dynamic that must be fixed. One-sided accountability is the defining attribute of a hierarchical relationship and the crux of disorientation and truth withholding. It is the mind-set that provides bosses the means for evaluating subordinate demeanor, methods, and results achieved without the subordinate being assured that his or her perceptions, views, and intentions are considered or that the boss's subjectivity and bias has been reviewed and checked. It's what allows bosses to walk away unscathed from firing the very employees they hired, selected for an assignment that failed, and for whom they were supposed to provide direction, oversight, and support. Something is wrong here, and we want to make sure you know the root cause.

The alternative is *two-sided accountability*, the highlight construct explored in this book. It leads to outcomes that every clear thinking organizational participant idealizes and which contrast dramatically with the negatives produced by hierarchical relationships and the hierarchical paradigm. Chapters 5, 6, and 7 sequentially analyze individual-to-individual, team, and organization-wide effectiveness problems with case examples to demonstrate how two-sided-accountable relationships readily lead to *straight-talk communication, authentic teamwork, aboveboard politics, esprit de corps*, and *stand-and-be-counted accountability*.

Chapter 3 initiates our transformational effort and campaign to have you change the logic you use when interacting with people at work. We ask, "Given the problems associated with hierarchical relationships, why haven't people smartened up? Why do they persist in forming the types of relationships that inevitably become losing propositions for themselves and the company?"

We present a set of human nature "truths" that everyone recognizes as valid but that most fail to utilize in their daily hierarchical thinking, truths that, if pointed out to them, they are inclined to dismiss as insignificant omissions, rationalizing, "I already know this." Our goal is to convince readers that they don't really "know" these essential "truths" until they are actually able to apply them. Why? Because when these "truths" are clearly represented in one's consciousness, the absurdity of hierarchical relationships becomes apparent. Hence the motive to overlook them. People who feel stuck, not knowing how to create a different type of interpersonal dynamic, resort to treating human beings nonhumanly.

Thus, this becomes the crucial chapter in convincing readers to break from set predispositions to engage in hierarchical relationships. Its goal is to make readers self-accountable for using human nature truths. Readers who take the lessons in this chapter to heart should acquire the capacity to self-invent alternative ways of responding to the hierarchical relationship dynamics that everybody encounters daily at work.

Chapter 4 addresses the second transformational imperative: changing how people think about political forces at work and the conduct of their political behavior. Without dragging in more "horror" stories, we argue that politics as usual can't get you where you need to go. Of course, the destination is two-sided accountability relationships.

We continue with a high-involvement case describing a salesman who, during a big storewide sale, comes in late without calling. We ask readers to respond as if they were the salesman's manager. Then we present a surprise answer that, in our experience with this case, few people think of and most quickly say is totally correct. We want readers to see how easily this is done when not using a hierarchical relationship mind-set.

Next we specify the precise elements of the thinking entailed in a paradigm in which the objective is two-sides-accountable partnering. We take pains to be thorough and precise, believing our precision pushes out the theory on relationships involving partnering to make it far more interesting and practically useful than the many platitudinous and moral treatments that have heretofore appeared in print.

The chapter culminates with a description of the greatest business partnering exercise we've ever seen or even heard about. It describes the proactive partnering advances made by a twenty-plus company consortium working to design and price Teledesic's

$14 billion, 150-satellite broadband "Internet In The Sky." Leading this project was a partnering genius whose efforts became industry legend.

Chapter 5 begins our effort to demonstrate systematically how two-sides-accountable thinking can improve everyday interactions at work. In this chapter we're interested in what an individual can unilaterally accomplish when engaging people inclined toward hierarchical relationships. Three short vignettes are presented as practical example illustrations of the immediate personal and organizational benefits an individual can receive from using a two-sided accountability mind-set. Then to anchor the reader's understanding and to provide confidence that the reader has it straight, we consolidate our discussion of two-sided accountability in a systematic presentation of underlying principles and tenets.

Chapter 6 applies two-sided accountability to people working in teams. It begins by indicting the American work culture's highly acclaimed but illusory notion of teamwork, the one that entails "snap-together" thinking. It's also the type of teamwork we find students using in the MBA courses we teach, which provides a neutral foil for criticizing how most people are inclined to operate at work. This critique allows us to state the positives gained from using this alternative, nonhierarchical model.

After a quick illustration of two-sided accountability teamwork, featuring a story about basketball great Magic Johnson, the chapter presents a longer case describing the highly effective teamwork practices used at The Home Depot, a company that wants to make team play its corporate DNA. It's instructive to review how the management of a large company that has been on a growth tear, doubling in size every four years, has created a training and development program using a two-sided accountability model.

Chapter 7 is about organization effectiveness and the corporation's need for two-sided accountability at the top. While one can point to successes, it's far easier to find organizational errors created by executives reasoning with one-sided accountability self-indulgence. We say "self-indulgence" because in most instances their actions are more driven by ego excesses than a desire to optimize team performance. Exposing these errors is the final stage setter for the radical proposal in Chapter 8 for reorienting people who haven't yet reasoned themselves through the boss domination problem.

The case for two-sided accountability at the top is made in Chapter 7 using examples that relate back to the "Internet In the Sky" case described in Chapter 4. In critiquing the power-denying tactics used by top executives, we ask, "Whose company is it, anyway?" This question lays the ground for a philosophical discussion to debunk the forked-tongued "We're working to improve shareholders' equity" answer so often provided by chief executives of large companies. The deeper issue, of course, is to benefit everyone in the company, which can happen only after top executives engage in *stand-and-be-counted* activities. We find it useful to draw a contrast in the reasoning used by executives directing start-up dot-coms and those directing mature corporations. The chapter concludes with a detailed discussion of the concrete actions that a boss committed to standing accountable can readily take.

Chapter 8 presents a radical proposal for fixing the structure, one that contrasts dramatically with what's mainstream in organizations today. The idea is to introduce two-sided accountability behavior to people who haven't yet acquired the mind-set so that they can enjoy the consequences and begin identifying with the result. We expect that people experiencing the benefits will acquire the rationale to produce more of that behavior on their own, thereby assuming a role in what we hope will become a chain reaction.

We begin with six quickly stated case vignettes that vividly point up glitches in the extant system to establish the need for a system like the one we are about to suggest. Then we state our proposal to change boss/subordinate relationships by infusion of a high degree of two-sided accountability. We describe how to fix accountability so that bosses who need to hold subordinates accountable also pay their accountability dues. Our proposal holds bosses accountable for positioning their reports to perform effectively. It promotes candor from below, real-time dialogue between the ranks and diminishments in ego indulgences.

Chapter 9 concludes our exposition by recognizing that the management and leadership lessons framed in this book will not be the same for all readers. People at different levels will benefit in different ways. Executives will learn how to change the system to promote honest, give-and-take interaction between bosses and subordinates within all levels of the ranks. Managers will learn how to reconfigure their relationships to better align with and support the people they want to lead. Subordinates will learn how to determine when it's safe to speak their minds and how to take more responsibility in creating those conditions. MBAs will learn how to size up potential employers when deciding which companies have the capacity to value their efforts and viewpoints at work.

This summary chapter revisits the five problems created by hierarchical relationships and presents a wrap-up contrasting the positives and negatives spelled out in the first two chapters and continuing throughout the book. Of course, the corporate goal is real teamwork, on-the-table politics, straightforward communications, two-sided accountability, and spirited participation up and down the line. Avoiding fairy-tale indulgences, we matter-of-factly conclude our case.

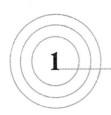

1

Recognizing the
Hierarchy Trap

Whether we're talking the boardroom at Procter & Gamble or the board of your PTA, you can count on hierarchy to screw things up. It's a paradox. On one hand, hierarchy provides people a basic orientation—it defines accountability and who has to answer to whom. On the other hand, it perverts relationships, bleeding candor and quality from almost every discussion that's held. As a feature of everyday work, hierarchy is a dimension people can't do without, but one that causes them not to do very well.

There's little question that hierarchy is the backbone of almost every well-functioning organization. It provides the architecture that structures a workforce. It designates authority, assigns responsibility, clarifies roles, and is a resource for settling jurisdictions and disputes. It is the primary mechanism for ensuring that work units set their compasses to corporate concerns and interact constructively with every group, even those units that appear uncooperative. Hierarchy causes people to be productive and efficient, keep their commitments, and stand accountable for errant actions. It authorizes leadership and insures respect for expertise. It specifies organizational purpose, stipulates functions, solidifies order, and provides control.

Hierarchy is part of growing up, learning the ropes, and being socialized. It's internalized in the lessons people learn about deferring to rank and observing rules. Those at the top of a hierarchy are allowed to dominate—to require, specify, and judge. Those lower down are expected to knuckle under, justify their actions, and stand accountable for results. People are taught that breaking ranks by ignoring hierarchy readily leads to anarchy, chaos, disorganization, and cascading ineffectiveness. And all of this is hardwired in each individual's thinking, even more so than what is specified in the books.

Every organization is layered with hierarchy; we're hard pressed to imagine one that works well without it. Usually, hierarchy flows from the person who is highest on the organization chart and authorized to make decisions. It also emanates from those with expertise, prestige, and image. It's even attributed on the basis of who is considered most socially and physically attractive. There's hierarchy in having money and friends in influential places. In fact, it's hard to think of any situation that doesn't come with multiple hierarchical overlays.

Hierarchy is essential; there's little doubt about that. Without it, work life would be likened to the Tower of Babel, for people would lack the means for reconciling divergent motives and differences in views. In fact, hierarchy is the chief mechanism for achieving corporate focus. Of course, one could always stop to take a vote, and some work groups operate that way. But once there's a vote, without someone to exercise hierarchical authority, integrity, focus, and efficiency are lost.

Notwithstanding the omnipresence of hierarchy and the essential needs it serves, one must also recognize that hierarchy is a cancer that causes human systems to close down. It almost always limits truth telling, authenticity, openness, and give-and-take exchange. In fact, nothing is more hazardous to the spirit of teamwork than hierarchy. Nothing more quickly attacks feelings of camaraderie and self-esteem. Hierarchy blocks originality and causes people to place efficiency and uniformity ahead of functional effectiveness and actual results. In problem solving, hierarchy creates convergence at the very moment problem solvers most need to step "out of the box" to open themselves to possibilities never before entertained. In relationships, hierarchy produces status-dominated thinking, testing-the-waters double-talk, and constraints to people acting sensibly. Predictably, it leads to participation by the numbers, filtered information, cover-ups, alienation, disorientation, anger, and depression.

Hierarchy damages morale and worse—it's dispiriting. Up, down, sideways, or diagonally, hierarchy obstructs, even negates, the possibility of straightforward, open and honest, candid conversations. In short, when it comes to relationships, hierarchy subtracts quality from every discussion and wisdom from the decisions determining the character of results.

HIERARCHY IS AN ORGANIZATION TRAP

The inability to differentiate between hierarchical *structure* and hierarchical *relationships* is precisely what makes hierarchy an organization trap. It needn't be a trap, and wouldn't be, if people realized the importance of making this distinction and had a way of keeping it in mind. As *structure*, hierarchy is the chain of command, the organization chart, and the road map that designates who is responsible for taking what action; who has the authority to make decisions and direct; and who is supposed to oversee and insist on corrective actions when specified results are not forthcoming. As *structure*, hierarchy is an organizational positive, providing the means for accountability and control.

But applied to *relationships*, hierarchy creates a negative dominance/subordination dynamic that works against an organization accomplishing its goals. Suddenly top-down, power-differentiated thinking appears in every interaction, and daily events take on a command-and-control demeanor in which people with more rank act as if they have the authority to require that people with less rank see and do things a certain way, regardless of individual predisposition. And as any parent with a teenager knows, a person not disposed to act as directed can evoke great resistance. Of course, grown-ups not so disposed, by virtue of personal reasoning, expert knowledge, skills possessed, or resources lacked, can marshal even greater resistance, or so it can seem when their reasoning is concealed.

Hierarchical *relationships* contrast with the way cooperating teammates and business partners with a common goal would interact if they were out to capitalize on each person's distinctive attributes and resources. By hierarchical *relationships*, we're talking most centrally about boss/subordinate interactions, but we're talking about other nonparity relationships as well. We're also talking about relationships contracting firms have with their suppliers, relationships between joint venture partners with unequal resources, and relationships firms have with independent contractors such as specialty lawyers, auditors, consultants, and travel agents. In every instance, when a relationship is engaged hierarchically, the company loses out. Thus, hierarchical thinking extrapolated to a business situation poses a burning-ember threat to any relationship that's combustible.

In this book we group the organization negatives associated with hierarchical relationships into five categories: **warped communication, corrupt internal politics, illusionary teamwork, personal dispiriting,** and **pass-the-buck accountability**. When it comes to people solving business problems and running organizations effectively, each of these negative dynamics represent significant obstacles to overcome.

We think these negatives are so blatant and onerous that as organization doctors called in to fix ailing relationships, we're constantly on the lookout for alternatives. We seek alternatives to the social conditioning that causes people to be intimidated by rank and stature to the point that they don't clearly say what they think or become self-inflated by their hierarchical stature to the point that they don't earnestly seek alternative views. And the changes had better come before too many more top-level executives and their companies get done in by what lower-level people think but don't dare say out loud and by what upper-level people hear but choose to overlook.

TWO-SIDED ACCOUNTABILITY PARTNERING IS THE ALTERNATIVE

Lately we've been using the term *two-sided accountability partnering* as the alternative to hierarchical relationships. It conveys the image of goodwill reciprocity leading to straightforward communications, aboveboard politics, authentic teamwork, esprit de corps, and the type of accountability that produces high-quality corporate results. *Two-sided* cues people to consider a reciprocal obligation to help one another in the pursuit of company goals. *Accountability* cues people to constrain self-interested pursuits that others might see coming at their expense. *Partnering* indicates a mutuality of interests that sets the stage for effective dialogue and interactive problem solving.

Two-sided accountability partnering contrasts with hierarchical relationships such as boss and subordinate, executive and manager, leader and follower, line and staff, strategist and operative, insider and outsider, central and peripheral, in the know and out of the flow, and so forth, which signal the dominance and superiority of viewpoints and ideas at the top. Two-sided accountability partnering communicates the image of collaborative action and people operating as real teammates—fully expressing themselves, filling in for one another, and jointly standing accountable for outcomes that benefit the enterprise as a whole.

As a means of illustrating the problems that accompany hierarchical relationships and the need for two-sided accountability, consider three revealing case studies. The first depicts the *hierarchy trap* that makes real teamwork impossible. It shows the ease with which hierarchical relationships get stuck in the logic of command-and-control and the teamwork difficulties that result. The second shows how hierarchical relationships warp communication and lead to a corrupt and manipulative brand of internal politics that can devastate an individual's career. The third displays the core dishonesty that shadows all hierarchical relationships and the ease with which positively motivated people become dispirited and self-delude. Taken together, the three cases begin our mapping of the destructive dynamics inevitable in hierarchical relationships and set the stage for appreciating the alternative logic that generates the remedies you'll be reading about in this book.

CASE 1

The Hierarchy Trap Leads to Illusionary Teamwork and Ineffective Problem Solving

Here's a case depicting a commonplace business problem that is almost always addressed with hierarchy, seldom with a satisfactory solution. It's a situation we encounter over and over again and is graphically illustrated in a recent experience where we observed a group of top-level executives of a prominent environmental cleanup company. They had invited us to watch them perform their allegedly acclaimed team approach to program oversight and project management.

> When we entered the meeting, the project manager was explaining his difficulties with the laboratory contracted to analyze the contamination level that remained in the ground their company was cleaning up. Provocatively he said, "Despite the fact that our company owns Analystat, we've reached the point where we have to fire them and bring in a lab that performs to schedule. We've got to," he grimaced. "We're in danger of losing money and, more importantly, losing the confidence of an established client." He recounted the details.

> "About a month ago we saw ourselves falling behind schedule. Anticipating upset, we called our client with a 'head's up.' We told him the lab was falling behind but not to worry, because they had given us assurances that they would shortly be on track. We offered to make up for lost time by working overtime at our own expense. At that point I had already called my counterpart at Analystat who assured me they'd be picking up the slack. I told him, 'You'd better.' Then I explained that overtime was now involved and we'd be billing them our extra costs.

> "A week later it was clear the lab still wasn't processing our volume, so I took up matters with my boss Al. Al told me to 'ratchet up the pressure,' which I did by placing a call to my

counterpart's director. The director said he was aware of the situation and assured me that the lab would be back on schedule within two weeks, which was fine with me. That would leave sufficient time to recover. But ten days later it appeared they still weren't gaining ground, so I went to Al, and he called that director. Unfortunately, another week has gone by, and to me it seems they are no closer to meeting their commitments than they were a month ago. That's how I concluded we should find another lab. Biting this bullet may help us earn back some of the credibility we've lost."

The project manager's account of Analystat's nonperformance seemed to anger just about everyone in the room. Suddenly, a red-in-the-face executive stood up and bolted swiftly toward the door announcing that he was leaving to call Analystat's president. He said, "I'm on their board. If these people intend to keep their jobs, they'd better start living up to their commitments." Everyone seemed relieved, as if suddenly they had their solution.

Half an hour later, our hosts asked for our impressions. Fascinated by the bankrupt logic we saw them using, we welcomed the opportunity to comment. On the other hand, we understood. Their response was driven by conventional hierarchical "wisdom."

We began by asking whether anyone saw alternatives to the way the project and program managers were handling their subcontractor problem. And for spice, we added, ". . . and the way Joe just dealt with Analystat's president?" No one had much to offer. Then we asked what people saw as the *methodology* underlying their attempts to solve the Analystat problem. Rhetorically, we offered that we saw it as problem solving through the use of a hierarchical relationship. We added that it seemed their backup methodology, for use when hierarchy failed, was the invocation of a more intimidating hierarchical relationship. We finished by declaring our belief that such a methodology can only lead to adversarial, close-minded, blaming relationships, introducing the irony of their acting adversarial with a business unit whose financial performance fell to the same bottom line as theirs.

Having their attention, we asked, "How might you proceed if you substituted a *'we can't succeed unless you succeed'* methodology for hierarchical muscle? What if you thought of Analystat as an operation you wanted to see make money and succeed, and dealt with their managers as if they were members of your own project team? Then their problems would be your problems, which clearly they are, for as you've been discussing, falling behind schedule is creating additional costs and negatively impacting your relationship with the client."

Our suggestion met with agreement, but it was obvious that, in the face of such a business betrayal, no one could envision what a nonhierarchical approach would entail. We offered, "If we thought of them as part of our team and the cause of our nonperformance, we'd be running to their facility asking to eyeball their problems and offering help in solving them. We'd want to see firsthand what they were facing, and we'd be willing to consider taking just about any action that might assist in correcting their nonperformance. For the moment we'd forget about organizational boundaries and absorb whatever costs emerged. Only after the problems were solved would we take time to sort out damages, culpability, and cross-charges. That would also be the time to examine for incompetence and to assess what's needed to avoid a "next time."

Our comments put the project manager on the defensive. He said, "What if the people at Analystat won't show us their problems?"

We responded, "Without knowing your relationship with them or the form their resistance might take, it's difficult to specify exactly how you might proceed. We'd want to say something like 'Hey! We're in this thing together and, speaking as your business partner, your denying us access is not OK. We can't succeed without you, so the problem isn't yours alone. Our partnership requires that you let us in. You certainly need our understanding, and, who knows, together we might stumble on a remedy. You can't be territorial when the corporation's profits and our relationship with a valued client are on the line.'"

While the others seemed to be enjoying the impromptu class, we were concerned that it was taking place at the project manager's expense. So we backed off without mentioning the possibility, obscured by the structure of the question, that the lab manager might actually welcome his viewing their problems and his help in solving them. Glancing around the room, we thought almost everyone else understood. We felt the project manager eventually would, too, but first he had to get past his embarrassment. He was feeling "one down," a hierarchical condition that blocks open-minded listening.

CASE 2

Hierarchical Relationships Lead to Warped Communication and Corrupt Internal Politics

Our next case highlights the political maneuvering, deception, and misuse of human resources that, in our experience, too often accompany hierarchical relationships. It shows that calling a relationship a "team effort" or a "business partnership" doesn't necessarily make it one. Our example centers on the relationship between a CEO named Bill and his hand picked choice to head operations, Lee. From the beginning, Bill had referred to Lee as his "business partner." Now if ever a situation could have been staged for a partnering relationship, this one was a natural. As you read along, note how words like *teamwork* and *partnering* were used to camouflage destructively competitive, hierarchical maneuvering. As is usually the case when hierarchical levels conflict, there's a loser and a bigger loser, the latter inevitably being the company.

Bill was the successor CEO to an entrepreneur who used stock swaps and reinvested profits to put together a conglomerate of like-industry companies big enough for listing on the New York Stock Exchange. At the corporation's beginning the marketplace was profit-friendly, and its share price rose. But, during the several years preceding Bill's hiring, the market turned dramatically downward, and an industry shakeout took place. Profit margins became so tight that most firms struggled to survive.

Bill's company was no exception. Survival and waiting for competitors to fold meant operating in and around the red with loss leaders required to keep their workforce occupied. Profitability was further burdened by the high interest rate paid for initial financing and the expense of working capital. Quickly, the price of the stock nose-dived from a high of thirty-five to six, and it went on to drop even lower.

The key to holding on was to redo the company's financial profile. Interest rates had come down, and refinancing at a lower rate was the quickest way to turn a positive cash flow. On the other hand, in order to get that financing, the company needed to show an immediate profit. Cutting costs to get that profit was Bill's immediate challenge, and he recognized the need for help.

Bill's competencies lay in political strategizing, coalition building, financial analysis, strategic planning, and presentations to customers and brokerage house investors. He was the big picture type with limited patience for managing people and attending to operating details. In fact, his best interpersonal skill appeared to be "schmoozing." He smiled a lot, took pains to appear personable, and had a flair for building up people when he needed them thinking positively. He exhibited many acts of personal and civic generosity that fed an affable, all-around good-guy image. Nevertheless, we also saw a person who was extremely self-focused, stubborn, and overly concerned with public face and who constantly substituted panache for substance.

To reduce costs, Bill quickly recruited an executive named Lee with a business background comparable to his own. Convincing the board to approve a half-million-dollar-a-year salary package, he told them, "I've finally found a fiscally tough COO to be my operations partner. This will allow me to concentrate on refinancing and bringing in new business." Then he told Lee, "This is just the beginning of our partnership. The next step is to move you up to president as I become chairman of the board." That exciting prospect persuaded Lee to leave a secure, albeit staid, job.

Almost from the beginning Lee complained that Bill was not cutting him sufficient authority to operate. This struck people as odd, because Bill had little patience for details and was known to practice "extreme delegation" management. Privately, Lee said, "Bill, you've got to stop micromanaging me." But that didn't seem to budge him. Lee couldn't figure out whether Bill was all hands-on or simply didn't trust him. As it turned out, it was the latter, although it took almost a year for Bill to sort out precisely what made him uncomfortable. While he felt it, he didn't have a handle on the fact that his and Lee's philosophies of management were dramatically different. People in the know wondered how Lee could go so long deferring to Bill, not confronting him about his lack of authority.

Lee wanted to centralize power, constrain local options, and install cost controls that were similar to the system used at his former company. In fact, everything he advocated was prototyped to how he operated there. People were irritated by his constant references to "how we did it at International." Always loquacious, Lee described his strengths as "I have a good understanding of where profits can be extracted and where leakage occurs. I know which human tendencies precipitate the leaks and what management needs to do to prevent them." To control against profit seepage, he argued, key corporate support functions such as Accounting, Human Resources, and Marketing should be realigned to report directly to him. Instead of stating directly that he favored a decentralized model, Bill would periodically counsel Lee, "Don't be in such a hurry to consolidate. Give the operating divisions time. Eventually they'll come around."

The resistance to Lee was great, but Bill never told him precisely what he wanted or coached him on how to build credibility. Instead of setting his business partner straight, Bill used hierarchy to constrain Lee's authority. Bill knew that people in the operations chain perceived Lee's "command-and-control orientation" to be ill suited to their business and antithetical to the autonomy they prized.

A couple of significant background factors contributed to Lee's entrenchment. The first was a management review he had received at his former company when he was given an elevation in title to mask a functional demotion. At that time he was told, "You spend too much time in the 'gray' and lack decisiveness." That may have been the case at the time, but no one saw evidence of anything like that once he took the job as Bill's COO. In fact, some joked, "If you want to see something that's quick, watch how fast Lee shoots from the lips."

The second factor was Bill's precarious political position with the board and his desire not to provoke Lee to break ranks. Setting an example, Bill always supported Lee with the board. He had to; he didn't want board members viewing his first significant hire as a half-million-dollar-a-year flop. When the director of human resources resigned, stating she couldn't do her job with integrity reporting to an overbearing COO, Bill maintained his support of Lee by not contradicting Lee's circle-the-wagons response that claimed her resignation stemmed from having a husband with a lower-status job who was uncomfortable with her travel. Thus, in the short run, the Bill/Lee partnership depended on Lee's looking like a contributor and making positive statements about the company's financial prospects.

It took the annual strategic planning process to force exposure of Bill's and Lee's differences. Bill was firmly lined up on the side of giving authority to operating unit heads so that he could hold them accountable for results. Lee, on the other hand, was pushing for uniform business practices, centralized controls, and "feet to the fire" management. Of course, this was the way he had always operated and was consistent with how he saw his mandate to get profits up by cutting costs.

Now seeing Lee as a liability, Bill used the strategic planning process to revamp the organization chart. Inserted underneath Lee were two strong-willed managers who, on the surface, appeared to be adding a level of hierarchy but who people in the chain could see as essential buffers. Quickly they caught on. Lee had been "elevated" to supernumerary. If Lee was reading the writing on the wall, no one in the company heard him divulge it. All that remained was the politically convenient moment when Bill could ease him out. That moment came three months later.

In response to the revamped organization chart, Lee began contrasting his role as "chief operating officer" with the roles of his two deputies, whom he called his "operating chiefs." Then Bill asked Lee to prepare a list of goals that he would take personal responsibility for accomplishing. Lee came back with three big-ticket items: he would create systems for lowering receivables, reduce indirect expense, and improve the format used for reporting financial results. Later on Bill confided, "While I didn't say anything at the time, from the beginning it was clear that Lee lacked the ability to achieve any one of his goals." Some onlookers got it right away. They joked that Bill had handed Lee a rope and sent him out to find a scenic view for the hanging.

Meanwhile, an "amazingly convenient" surge of business and profits occurred, just in time to establish the financial profile needed for refinancing. However, this spurt was immediately followed by a business "downturn" that caused the next two quarters to be spent deep in the red, causing many to wonder about the bookkeeping. Discussing the financial downturn with the newly elected board chairman—the second one in a year—Bill said, "I guess the time has come to cut the expensive staff and managers that our business can no longer support." He added, "Of course, such a fact will not be credible without taking a hit or two at the top." Then he offered up Lee, explaining that Lee was failing miserably with the three assignments he had taken on.

"Lack of progress on your special projects" was the story Bill took to Lee. Lee protested, saying he had been given six months to achieve his objectives and only three had elapsed. Bill countered with, "If you leave now we can give you a year's salary and a positive reference. After all, everyone understands that downsizing and politics at the top are the no-fault grounds for involuntary dismissals these days. If you fight us, I can't predict what we'll be able to do." Demoralized, Lee took the half million dollars. He also sold himself on the illusion that by going quietly and papering his actions with a constructive appearance he could retain the image of positive contributor. Nevertheless, everyone in upper management realized what had transpired. Several took it as an object lesson of what could happen to them either at this company or elsewhere.

Despite a profusion of words, at no time did we see anything resembling the type of honesty and respect for differences that one expects from a true partnering relationship. Instead we saw a hierarchical relationship enabling an insecure CEO to use deception to cover over a personnel mistake. Hierarchical relationship protocol caused Lee to go a year without comprehending that his and Bill's managerial orientation were 180 degrees apart. We can only speculate about the role hierarchy played in achieving the positive quarterly results that paved the way for enterprise saving refinancing. Understandably, we never heard anyone openly debate whether this was a business or spreadsheet accomplishment.

Hierarchy allowed Bill to perform face work on Lee and Lee to perform face work on himself. Politically insensitive and isolated from the views of others, he was hierarchically deferential to the point that he got taken in by a partnering scam. Coalition building, collusion, and manipulation led to Lee's demise. Bill took all the power, even when Lee was issuing directives to levels below, while the two of them exchanged goodwill to maintain the illusion of harmony.

CASE 3

Dishonesty Shadows All Hierarchical Relationships Leaving Participants Dispirited and Self-deluding

Whether we're talking top executives or recent university graduates, most people come to work wanting to be part of "the team." It would seem that all a newcomer needs to convert positive intention to behavior is a little guidance and reinforcement. Certainly this is the thinking that most executives possess when starting a new job or new assignment, and it's what most young people believe when entering corporate life.

But something happens. Newcomers "learn the ropes." They encounter people who appear to be "bad guys," and out of what they perceive as a necessity, they take "precautions" that ultimately undermine their instincts to be team players.

Of course, most alleged corporate bad guys also began their careers expecting to be team players. But their survival and progress in the system have required political safeguards that alienated coworkers. Their words have been experienced as deceitful, image managing double-talk. Their actions have been seen as manipulative, heavy-handed, and backstabbing. While most of them would say that their behavior has been necessary, few can clearly remember how they got into such a mode. Consider the situation faced and survival lessons learned by one of the brightest and most positively intentioned engineers we've ever met when, in her first major managerial assignment, she attempted to express her genuine partnering spirit and team-play mind-set. Keep in mind, each of the people thwarting her positive efforts used to be a good guy, a team player just like herself.

We met Karen when the idea of being a partner and teaming up with people was front and center in her mind. Recruited directly out of college, Karen had worked for her company ever since. That was eight years ago, and recently she had been advanced to the fast track. Now she had a high profile managerial assignment, and the company was funding her time and tuition in UCLA's "MBA Program for the Fully Employed." Hearing about our work, she called for a consultation. Teaming up was getting her down.

Karen described how she had been made assistant director for a large technical unit that serviced and repaired sophisticated electronic equipment. She characterized her Director as "the mentor type: a person who shares departmental leadership by involving me in all facets of management and operations." Listing her unit's problems, she said, "When it comes to production, scheduling, quality, or costs, things couldn't be worse." Using impressive MBA nomenclature she explained the situation: "We're doing a poor job managing our growth. We don't keep time commitments, and we make too many errors. We're constantly in crisis playing catch-up and needing to hire more people than we had planned for. Then, because we're behind, we don't have time to do a decent job training those we bring on. Making matters worse, throughout the company people are worried about downsizing. And senior management has exploited this insecurity. They've replaced high-paid supervisors with less expensive lead technicians who are no longer paid hourly; they receive a fixed salary. All of this was decided by higher-ups without consulting my boss or any other midlevel manager. The result is demoralization and a deep-seated distrust toward all of us in management.

"So I'm left with a poor to no-leadership situation beneath me. The new unit heads and technical supervisors have yet to receive supervisory and managerial training, and we're hard pressed to provide it since we're under the gun to keep expenses down. And, of course, our emphasis is on catching up."

We asked Karen, "What are you going to do?" She responded, "I'm going to tell my unit heads to go all-out

superhuman to catch up and create some time for training."
We responded, "Before doing that, why not ask them for
their view of the situation?" "There's no need to do that,"
she said, "I already know how they see it. They favor training first and then production, but we already know that this
is totally unacceptable to upper-level management. Asking
them will serve no constructive purpose." We replied, "The
theory suggests that the best way out of your morale and
confidence crisis is to partner up with the people you work
with—up, down and sideways." Skeptically she rebutted,
"After being sold down the river, I can't see the unit heads
and technicians going for that one again."

To her pessimistic view we responded, "Karen, it's not the
people below you we're worrying about right now—it's you
and the treatment you and your director are receiving from
your upper-level managers. We see you about to betray yourselves by being positive with workers and getting your own
hopes up in reaction to a problem that your top management
has caused. From what you've described, it's not clear that
your management will back you if, through your earnestness,
you succeed in convincing your workforce to go all-out.
Before talking with them, see if you can get your uppers to
buy in. You don't want to betray lower levels again by promising solutions to problems your management refuses to have."

Noticing that we had run way beyond the allotted time, we invited Karen back for another conversation but failed to set a
date. When we didn't hear from her, we put in a call that she
failed to return. It was several months before we heard from
her again. She reappeared enrolled in a leadership course we
were teaching. A couple of weeks later she asked for a meeting.

We began that meeting by asking, "What's up? How are things
going?" Karen replied, "While production problems continue,
my director Paul and I have now created bonds of trust and
openness with our unit heads." She said, "We did so by taking
a page out of your book. We went around, told them we were
interested, and just plain listened. We've now spoken with all
of our unit heads and lead workers as well as many of our two

hundred-plus technicians. From them we've learned how our organization is structured to make it difficult for people to do what seems right or even to just make positive suggestions. We've discovered that we're much too centralized. Few seem to have the big picture, and no one has an accurate idea of what our customers say they need. In response Paul and I are now holding what we call a 'Tuesday Open Lunch,' a time for anyone who wants to discuss improvements and the big picture. The problem is that despite improving relationships, we have yet to change anything substantive."

Karen went on, "Paul and I have now held a couple of very disappointing conversations with his boss, Stan, and we're really frustrated. We know precisely what needs to be done, but Stan is blocking us. At the first meeting we simply described what we had learned and the remedies we wanted to take, but Stan was totally negative. He never even said what he didn't like. In fact, I still don't know. The least he could have said was, 'You've got some good ideas here, and these are my problems with what you suggest.' But instead he went command-and-control saying, 'I don't want you proceeding this way,' and completely killed our motivation. All we did was present him a plan for collaborating with the only people who can improve our deteriorating situation!"

Continuing, Karen said, "We left that meeting in a state of shock. But our disbelief about what happened was too great, so we decided to schedule another session. That one was much more polite and surface-friendly, but still we made no headway. Stan was positive and had some good ideas, but he never once engaged our premise of letting the people who perform the work be involved in the thinking. I still don't see how you can go in with a modern management theory and twice have the boss tell you back 'I don't care.'"

At this point we apologized for not being clearer in our initial discussion. We said, "This bears on a point we tried to make last time. To us it sounds like Stan hasn't bought your framing of the problem. He's working off a different formulation. It sounds as if he believes you need to exert greater control of your workforce while you are out trying to partner up with them."

Karen responded, "Oh, I heard you clearly enough, but I didn't like your message. Now I have no alternative but to face what's going on." We replied, "It appears as if you and your direct reports have similar problems. Both of you are receiving visuals of your management being concerned, but you are getting lip service without real partnering. Of the two varieties, we prefer your position with Stan, because at least you accurately know what's being done to you. We're afraid that the openness and goodwill you've extended to the people reporting to you may cause them to feel betrayed once again."

Searching to find any avenue of hope, we asked, "Who does Stan report to? What's that person's rank, and what's he or she like?" We were exploring the treacherous idea of an end run. Perhaps Karen, a female engineer in whom the company was investing to the tune of an expensive MBA, could get the big boss's ear.

Karen responded, "Stan reports to Phil, the division president. And the best way to describe Phil is that he's a clean-desk type. He's ex-military, likes order in the ranks, and likes to say 'Yes, sir' to his boss. If you're suggesting that he might be an open ear, I don't think it's going to happen." After hearing her description, we didn't, either. In our minds the prognosis was "terminal."

A week later Karen was back, this time upset to the point of tears. She told us, "The other shoe just dropped. Two days ago Stan confided that upper management has completed a deal to move our technical operations to a recently closed military base in Indiana. He says we've got a captive community there with a skilled, unemployed workforce that gladly will work for lower wages. And, to boot, the situation comes with tax credits. He thinks he's a genius. In one fell swoop the company lowers its costs and rids itself of a major morale problem." Reflecting for a moment, we added, "And they seem to have found a way to keep their dominance model intact." In response, Karen told us, "I'm so upset. While we were going all out to win people over by teaming up with them, our management was negotiating to close down our operation. Now we're pledged to secrecy lest our workers get wind of this and begin quitting before we're finished with them." Full of emotion, she paused.

Continuing, Karen said, "I have worked hard for this company, and I want to be loyal. But apparently that's not the relationship they want with me." For us that translated as "How do you partner with people who won't partner with you?" We kept quiet; there was nothing for us to say. Karen was receiving on-the-job reality training. It was one of those sobering moments where you begin to see what previously you didn't want to see about the way a hierarchical relationship works.

Several days later Karen dropped by to tell us that she had decided to look for another job. We liked her conclusion. She hadn't given up looking for a system that worked differently. She hoped to find a situation where real teamwork was possible, where she could avoid taking the route that her company predecessors had taken when their corporate experiences brought them to the point of making peace by buying in.

Certainly we could see the logic of the path taken by executives at Karen's company. They had the opportunity to trade an expensive workforce for a motivated new group that would accept even lower wages and tax credits that would offset the costs of training. Nevertheless, we left Karen's saga wondering how long it will take for management's newly found human assets to begin feeling like the former group. How long would it take for them to fathom that they are in an "object" relationship, seen as human resources to be deployed and moved around to fit management's objectives, despite a profusion of words about their essentiality and membership on the company team?

SUMMARY

We've presented three cases to illustrate the destructive dynamics produced by hierarchical relationships, even when "team play" and "partnering" terms are used. Each is an instance of people exercising hierarchical power, comprehending neither the competitive forces their actions provoke nor the alternatives at their disposal. In each situation the participants easily rationalized their actions as essential to the corporation.

The first case depicts a line of managers stuck in a hierarchical trap, futilely attempting to create teamwork using the logic of command-and-control. Graphically, it illustrates how people caught up in hierarchical thinking have a difficult to impossible time seeing how to team up and partner with one another. Above all, it demonstrates a *without-exception principle* that we'll emphasize over and over again in this book: **whenever hierarchical relationships flourish, the company loses out.**

The second case presents a deeper view of the command-and-control dynamics that accompany any relationship steeped in hierarchy. Dramatically, it illustrates **the ease with which hierarchical relationships lead to warped communication and a corrupt and manipulative brand of internal politics that can devastate an individual's career.** It demonstrates the importance of not being taken in by illusions of team play and partnering and of figuring out whether someone's partnering talk is actually being walked.

The third case illustrates **the core dishonesty that shadows all hierarchical relationships and the ease with which positively motivated people delude themselves.** It shows how the tension of being part of a teamwork sham can become so great that it leaves an individual with but two alternatives: to become depressed and dispirited or to go into denial about his or her conspiratorial role. Our student was dispirited; her bosses were in denial. We think denial is a particularly amazing response when you consider that almost every hierarchical superior is a junior to someone else. As a superior he or she knows how often reality gets spun for consumption by the ranks below. As a subordinate he or she knows how often facts are withheld and personal perspectives suppressed in order to self-promote the image of good guy and loyal team member.

Why do people persist in reasoning and acting hierarchically? For many reasons, starting with a very basic and elementary one. Hierarchical relationships feel like a contour fitting baseball cap so comfortable and familiar that a person loses track of having it on.

It's a relationship that's automatic. We've been socialized in a culture where people in power are able to dominate to the point that the dominated secretly dream of eventually having the same type of power, all under the guise of issuing directives that promote corporate effectiveness and efficiency. None of the three cases described achieved that result.

We are guessing that each of these situations feels familiar to you—less for their specifics, more for their runaway dynamics and logic. We're also guessing that many readers will identify with feelings of being both a hierarchical relationship perpetrator and a hierarchical relationship victim. These are but the beginning of a collage of cases that will illustrate what's off about the way relationships get conducted at work. They introduce our explanation of what's needed for teaming up and partnering with people above, alongside, and below you in any hierarchy.

Our overarching goal is to reset relationships currently structured for hierarchical mischief. We want to provide insight into the dynamics provoked by hierarchy and to explain what's needed for making the transition to a much different mind-set, one with a reciprocal accountability orientation. We're out to show you how to redirect the hierarchical, command-and-control reasoning that blocks you and your organization from delivering more of what people require to operate at peak effectiveness. In Chapter 8, we propose a corporate solution for modernizing relationships aimed at systemically righting what we find wrong.

Making the transition to a two-sides-accountable mind-set requires adjusting your perspective on human nature to include what probably you almost know but fail to utilize in daily interactions. We know adjustments are needed. Otherwise, you would already possess a sufficiently deep appreciation of the havoc wreaked by hierarchical relationships to put more effort into avoiding them. Modifying your perspective will allow you to uncover teamwork opportunities that are there for the taking, regardless of how others are initially inclined. Minimally, you'll be able to clarify the force field in which you are operating and learn ways of taking relationships to a more open and candid place. However, like all modes of operating, no format or plan works with all people or in all situations. That's where more consciousness of what's going on comes in. We think increased awareness of how candor, truthfulness, and robust give-and-take are perverted by hierarchy will prove a practical tool.

Thus, in addition to providing you an alternative to hierarchical relationships that is far more strategic for you and your company, we think exposure to cases describing hierarchical relationships will cause you to reflect on like situations that you have experienced and equip you for sidestepping hierarchical entrapments. The fray is taking place. We all need ideas for avoiding it so that we don't fall victim or worse. What could be worse? "Worse" is falling into dominating or subordinating patterns with people on whom you'll want to depend, either presently or in the future, for high-integrity, straight-talking teamwork.

2

The Core Problem Is One-Sided Accountability

We grouped the problems associated with hierarchical relationships into five categories: **warped communication, corrupt internal politics, illusionary teamwork, pass-the-buck accountability,** and **personal dispiriting**. As you may have noticed in the three cases related in Chapter 1, these problems overlap, each one feeding the others. One of the problems, **pass-the-buck accountability,** was more alluded to than described, so here we begin with a brief case to illustrate its dynamics. It's a notorious story, one you've been reading about for years. It concerns the management of Los Angeles's finest, the LAPD.

CASE 1

Pass-the-Buck Accountability

The Los Angeles Police Department (LAPD) found itself in yet another crisis when the media exposed right-wing vigilante actions taken by rogue cops planting evidence and giving false testimony against people they suspected in unsolved crimes. In the aftermath of what became known as the Rampart Street Precinct scandal, the federal government threatened to step in with management mandates and substitute leaders. Vigorously resisting were Police Chief Bernard Parks, whose leadership role would be reduced to that of a functionary, and the five-member Police Commission, appointed by the mayor with City Council

ratification to provide oversight. Opposed to government inter-
ference, these parties requested recommendations from an independent, blue-ribbon panel of citizens composed of business
leaders, experts, and noteworthy lawyers.

Well into their investigation, in the stage of preparing recommendations, panel representatives called asking us to serve as
consultants—an invitation we initially accepted. But when told
how the panel was construing the problem and about constraints
on access to panelists, we backed out. We believed that the situation was already sunk and that we could achieve more by expressing our viewpoints as interested citizens. As framed, the
assignment asked us to think about how the information exchanged between officers on duty and their direct supervisors
together with after-the-fact statistical data could be modified to
better alert supervisors when a specific officer acted improperly.

Any moviegoer knows that Los Angeles's police have a history
of suspect performance and mismanagement. *Chinatown, L.A.
Confidential,* and every Raymond Chandler novel have depicted a
history of serious flaws. On the other hand, the 1960s TV series
Dragnet and the 1970s series *CHiPS* have portrayed some ad-
mirable qualities. But the department's recent history has been
notoriously scandal ridden. In fact, our liaison handed us a copy
of the report written by a task force headed by former secretary of
state Warren Christopher that was prepared in the aftermath of
the 1991 Rodney King beating and police overreaction to ensuing
citizen rioting. That report proposed a long list of management
reforms aimed at both immediate and long-term improvements.
Five years later, in 1996, a panel of special counsels reviewed the
implementation of the Christopher Commission recommendations, concluding that the report had been largely ignored.
Now, four years later, the very same problems taken up by the
Christopher Commission had resurfaced in the form of another
scandal with yet another panel formulating recommendations.

Thinking the problem might, in part, be generic, we asked our
liaison, "Which cities are known for having well-managed police? What police department is known as having an exemplary

management system in place?" The response came back, "With two exceptions, there are no well-managed, exemplary police departments. The first exception is Pittsburgh, where things got so bad that the Department of Justice (DOJ) took over, and the second is the Los Angeles County Sheriff's department." Inquiring about the latter, we learned that recommendations based on their successes were considered suspect by LAPD managers. When we asked why, we received a long-winded explanation that in our minds boiled down to an analog of the "not invented here" syndrome common in the engineering profession. Apparently, operating in such close proximity produces resistance to using a "competitor's" template.

At this point, we began to fear what every member of the panel must have feared after reading the "Five Years Later" report: time spent trying to figure out improvements would be effort wasted. Trying to get to the heart of the matter, we began tracking for accountability. We must have asked twenty questions aimed at understanding why the spotlight was on errant officers and not further up the line. If the panel stuck to its mandate, the most they would accomplish would be to push accountability up one echelon from officers to first level supervisors. We thought, "Hey, how about the chief? He's been in that system for thirty years; how can he point the finger downward? How about the captains, lieutenants, and sergeants? How about the mayor and the police commissioners he appointed?" We even thought about the editorial watch-guard duties of the *Los Angeles Times* and other media following the police beat. "Isn't there anyone or any institution besides the DOJ that has the ultimate charge to provide oversight and ensure that recommended improvements are being implemented and that the system is operating with integrity?"

Probing each avenue, we began to understand why the panel was focusing on the lowest supervisory level. Apparently the bodies that govern and lead the police department lack a procedure for working together. We could not identify anybody below the feds in a position to insist that authorities and power relationships be changed. Analogous to rogue cops looking for vulnerable citizens to take the fall for each hit, the panel was looking for an unprotected management system to improve. In this instance they were out to extract more accountability from first level supervisors, people who obviously lacked the training, authority, and power to change the superstructure, and whose track record in identifying and stamping out corrupt cops was blatantly suspect.

It's not worthwhile to go into all the details about Los Angeles's weak mayoral system, the authority of the governmental bodies above, or the role of the press in oversight and as guardians of civil rights. Even Chicago, with its strong mayoral system, failed to make the well-managed cop shop list provided to us. The overriding point is that here's an accountability system where the buck passing never stops, with each management echelon having both the motivation and the means for blaming others whenever a troublesome situation comes up. At the structural level, the hierarchical chart and chain of command is confused—people with responsibility possess fragmented authority that is insufficient for initiating corrective action and systemic change. In short, there's no one with enough authority to stipulate systemic revisions and stand up to self-interested factions that resist.

At the relationship level it's every group looking out for itself, and individuals seeking a safe haven from blame depending on hierarchical, command-and-control logic for protection. People do what they are told, fearing that disagreeing will get them labeled insubordinate and personally responsible for "the problem." The result is minimal dialogue among people in various positions up and down the chain of command and little, if any, cross-echelon problem solving. These dynamics were apparent to us when we read a confidential report prepared by LAPD internal investigators, which we thought obfuscated upper-echelon accountability and failed to conclude with a fix. Only the DOJ appeared to know what was needed, but their solutions were being resisted as a jurisdictional, local governance defeat.

Typically pass-the-buck accountability favors hierarchical uppers, with subordinates blamed for what goes awry. Hierarchical relationships allow bosses to walk away unscathed from firing the very employees they hired, selected for an assignment that failed, and for whom they were supposed to provide training, direction, oversight, and support. This allows bosses to get ahead while their subordinates fail. Former LAPD Chief Willie Williams survived the aftermath of the King beatings and exhortations levied by the Christopher Commission report. And in all likelihood Chief Bernard Parks and Mayor Richard Riorden will continue to get good press, even after the Rampart panel reports in.

THE PEOPLE INVOLVED KNOW HIERARCHY IS A PROBLEM BUT SEEM UNABLE TO EXTRICATE THEMSELVES FROM THE TRAP

At the core of the problems created by hierarchical relationships is one individual's domination of another. This is what blocks people with knowledge from making a contribution; this is what enables people with power to isolate themselves from resources that could help their company. People on top set the structure and compose the chart believing that this provides people below them sufficient security and authority to speak their minds openly. But they don't; in fact, most lowers feel that leveling and straight talking comes with such perilous consequences that they have little recourse but to play it safe.

It's a dumb situation that needs changing. More than ever, you want to see responsible parties exercising their decision making authority with maximum intelligence and 360-degree perspective and this requires input from the ranks. We're living in a new era where any one person's view is all but guaranteed to be insufficient. It's a technologically complex, globally operating, culturally diverse, subcontractor-dependent, customer contact point–sensitive, information-abundant, modern organizational world, where more and more people have distinctive perspectives on what's good for the company that you'd like to see considered when important decisions are made.

Unfortunately, you can't count on essential perspectives to be adequately communicated upward to allow people at the top to operate intelligently. When input from the ranks is provided, it seldom gets presented straight. When input is not provided, people on the top seldom do a good enough job seeking it out. Why? Because most people automatically extrapolate from hierarchical structure to hierarchical relationships and, in the process, they disorient themselves. People on the top become self-inflated by their role and organizational stature, believing that they know more than they do, while people lower down suffer from intimidation, believing they lack the power to set uppers straight.

The result is a kind of institutionalized schizophrenia in which bosses forget about how they withhold when conversing with the people to whom they report. The games they play may be subtle, but they are the same ones their subordinates play with them. There's "spin the story," "withhold some facts," "flatter the leader," "watch me maneuver," "calculated version," "ingratiating commentaries," and a general playing up to bias and ego. As a boss they adopt the self-sealing belief that they can spot insincerity; as a subordinate they act as if their self-interested maneuvering defies discovery.

For an example of what we're describing and some of the games that are played, we draw on a situation created when a friend of ours performed an outrageous act. Inadvertently, he exposed the disorientations of a self-inflated chairman/CEO and of a high-ranking subordinate who was reluctant to level with him. His action presented the subordinate a golden opportunity to set his CEO straight on an issue that the subordinate later said needed corporate correcting. On review, however, it's not clear whether the act engaged in by our friend was more outrageous than the self-indulgence of the CEO or the cover-up, business-as-usual actions taken by his high-ranking subordinate. Relating the story allows us to illustrate the overly indulgent treatment too many bosses receive.

CASE 2

Who Performed the Most Outrageous Act?

Leaving the Keystone Foundation's prestigious environmental awards gala, our friend walked up to one of the three awardees, the CEO of a major oil company whom he had not previously met, extended his hand, shot him the broadest smile, and, addressing him by his first name as if he had known him for years, said, "Congratulations on the award, Larry, and, by the way, that was the worst *fuckin'* speech I ever heard." Then, while shaking the stunned CEO's hand, he held out his university business card and just stood there. We watched the incredulous CEO thank him and pocket his card. By this time other "well-wishers" were lining up, and there was no way for the two of them to continue their "conversation."

If it weren't that our friend's depiction paralleled our own feelings, we would have written off his impropriety to the wine. But if our friend was intoxicated by wine, then this CEO was intoxicated by his hierarchical position. To this day we can think of no alternative explanation for the self-indulgence we witnessed that night. In a captive room of more than a thousand, including a half-dozen U.S. senators and a score of congressmen, this man spent twelve to fifteen minutes on a recipient's speech rambling self-indulgent non sequiturs as a transparent vehicle for publicly acknowledging his friends.

A week later our friend received a phone call from Steve Whatever, who introduced himself as vice president of governmental relations for the CEO's firm. He said, "I was standing next to 'the chairman' when you engaged him at the awards banquet last week and overheard what you said. I'm calling to inquire whether the chairman inadvertently offended a group or cause that you represent?" Our friend replied, "No, not at all. Only my sensibilities were offended."

The vice president asked, "Which sensibilities?" Our friend responded, "Well, what did *you* hear *your* chairman say?" Vice president: "Oh, I've been with the chairman twenty-two years, and it's gotten to the point where I just tune into the music, I already know all the words." Friend: "Well, let me tell you what I heard. I heard your chairman waste fifteen minutes of the lives of a thousand people on self-indulgent personal networking. There were no ideas, just five people who got to hear their names mentioned to a crowd of distinguished people whose companies kicked in $500 to $1,000 a plate so that they could mingle with congressional and industry heavyweights and celebrate environmental do-gooding."

Defensively, the vice president responded, "Well, what's to say about the environment to a crowd like that? It's like preaching to the choir, isn't it?" Outraged, our friend blasted back, "Are you kidding? Take me for example. As a management professor I'm interested in learning how a company operating an environmentally aggressive business such as oil production walks the line between shareholder return and taking care of nature. I would genuinely value his perspectives as an object lesson to discuss with MBA students. And, given a little time, I'll think of additional topics that would be worthwhile for that audience to hear your chairman address."

The vice president replied, "That's really good. I like that. Between you and me, he does this all the time. I'll tell him what you said. He ought to be able to learn something important from it." But, three days later when he received a copy of the letter the vice president wrote the CEO to describe his investigation, our friend could find no substantive comments critiquing what he objected to in the chairman's speech. The letter merely mentioned that he had held a follow-up conversation with the person who had critically commented on the chairman's speech and that he judged the critic's intentions to be constructive. Written deferentially, the letter made no reference to the chairman's self-indulgence or misuse of station and power. It didn't even mention the positive suggestion our friend had made about how the chairman's acceptance could have communicated something meaningful.

We have reflected back on this incident many times, for the position taken by the vice-president got our goat. Perhaps a follow-up conversation was held in which this executive told his chairman the now "shared truth." If it was, that lesson was not apparent in a subsequent speech we heard that chairman make about one year later.

WE'RE TALKING HIERARCHICAL *RELATIONSHIPS*, NOT HIERARCHICAL *STRUCTURE*

We're at a point where it's useful to revisit the distinction between structure and relationships. Hierarchical *structure* is the top-down map that determines who is authorized to make what decision, who controls which resources, and who has to account to whom. It is epitomized by the chain of command, buck-stops-here authority one finds in the military. In contrast, hierarchical *relationships* pertain to the top-down, power-deferential ways people think, talk, and behave with one another when chain-of-command authorities are imported into the problem-solving discussion people hold prior to deciding which action to take. In a hierarchical relationship, the value and impact of an opinion and the directness with which an opinion is expressed are significantly impacted by the hierarchical ranks of the participants.

When a relationship is hierarchical, you can count on the organization losing out. One or both parties may come out all right, but, inevitably, the organization takes it on the chin. We have no quarrel with a hierarchical relationship in which the person with the most expertise gets a bigger say, as long as the lack of parity is limited to the domain of that person's knowledge and not extrapolated more generally to cover other topics and all interactions. For example, many knowledge workers take an appropriately assertive, even intellectually aggressive, stance when holding discussions with a boss on a topic of their expertise. However, we become alarmed whenever we observe a globally hierarchical relationship that makes it possible for uppers to categorically reject and submerge the opinions and beliefs of lowers without seriously or open-mindedly engaging them.

The dynamic that allows uppers to categorically reject whatever they don't want to hear and its cost to the company is apparent in the following short case. It's an opportunity for you to put on your consultant's hat to consider how you would handle a like situation and what you would advise.

SHORT CASE

The Boss Who Wouldn't Deliver Needed Help

Envision yourself a management professor teaching midlevel managers at the Anderson School of the University of California, Los Angeles (UCLA). Upon completion of a class, a student approaches you with a question. Explaining that he's an HR manager working for a leading Japanese car manufacturer, he says, "I'd like your thoughts about a work problem that keeps me up at night." Sensing a high level of upset, you patiently hear him out. Consider what he had to say and how you would answer two rudimentary questions: What is his problem? and What advice do you have for him?

The manager explains, "I'm in charge of recruiting, training, and supporting personnel for our newly built North American Parts Distribution Center, which has been up and running for six months. When the center opened, Tokyo management predicted they'd start at 30 percent capacity and, over a one-year period, gradually increase to 100 percent. However by the end of the second month, demand was so great we were running two shifts at 100 percent capacity. People were being pressured to work 'voluntarily' six days a week and overtime as well. On an optional basis, some occasionally worked a seventh day."

Continuing, he says, "Nothing has changed, and the situation couldn't be worse. Our personnel are undertrained, stressed out, and can't be augmented due to overseas management setting rigid limitations on the number of permanent employees we're allowed to hire. The center is suffering high rates of turnover, while absenteeism and shipment errors are increasing. You can't imagine how many hours I spend each and every week interviewing and hiring 'temporary employees' who must be pressed into service without time for sufficient training."

You ask, "So what are you doing about it?" He responds, "I've just finished tabulating the data, and I'm preparing a report that I'll be sending just as soon as it's finished in the overnight pouch that goes to my line boss in Japan, probably tomorrow."

OK, what *is* the manager's problem? What advice do you have for him?

To us, there's no question about it. The core problem faced by this manager is his confinement in a hierarchical relationship. How else do you account for his going so long being unable to take the only action that made sense to him? Holding an open discussion he might have said something like, "Please either explain why you won't allow me to do what seems so reasonable or provide a feasible solution." Resorting to writing a time-consuming report meant he hadn't gotten anywhere discussing it. We saw his use of numerical data as an act of political intimidation aimed at painting his boss into a corner where he had to go along with what this manager long ago had concluded. Likewise, we saw his spur-of-the-moment outreach for our "expert concurrence" as further intimidation backup. Grasping what he was up to, we feared for his political safety. We reasoned, perhaps he'll succeed in winning this battle, but that doesn't guarantee he'll be out of the war. There's nothing like losing a power struggle to a subordinate to inspire a hierarchically oriented boss to exercise more power.

This case illustrates several of the most common problems spawned by hierarchical relationships, such as apparent disregard for the other person's reality, lack of candor, and power pressuring. Here we've got a boss denying that he's in a situation that requires action he doesn't want to take. We've got a blocked subordinate on a crusade to accomplish what he feels is organizationally "correct." This is precisely the type of situation that can never be resolved harmoniously by two people not being straight with one another.

Recognizing the hierarchical relationship, we advised, "Make your report simple; your boss already knows where you stand. Briefly reference the recruiting, training, and quality problems you face, and merely provide him your statistics. Then, using appropriate nomenclature ask, 'Boss, what do you want me to do?' Withhold your suggestions for increasing manpower with regular hires, and cool it on reciting the justifying rationales you, no doubt, have artfully prepared to force your boss into endorsing the obvious actions you want to take. If someone is going to get the credit for fixing this intolerable situation, apparently it's got to be your boss."

Why did we advise him to withhold his suggestions? Because the required actions were "no-brainers" that any reasonable person would come to when exposed to the facts this manager had stated long ago. After all, this was six months into a situation that was present from day 1, more than enough time for a boss who wanted to engage local management's problems either to have done so or to have explained why he could not. "Scientific" documentation might force the boss to go along, to the extent he had the latitude to do so, but it would not be responsive to the forces at Tokyo Corporate that prevented him from endorsing the actions our student initially brought up months ago. To engage this situation forthrightly, a nonhierarchical relationship was required.

When functioning in the context of a hierarchical relationship, pushing the boss can prove costly. It risks cueing the boss that you are not the "team player" he wants around. We were worried that backed into a corner, the boss might decide to recast the problem to make it appear that the ugly numbers the HR manager gathered were caused more by an insufficient local effort than by a misguided corporate plan.

HIERARCHICAL RELATIONSHIPS BREED CORRUPTION IN THE NAME OF SAYING THINGS ARE UNDER CONTROL

If hierarchical relationships are so detrimental to the company's well-being, then why do people make them their default setting? This is the basic question, and the answer is surprisingly elementary. People make hierarchical relationships the default setting because they want to get ahead in a system they believe is *politically corrupt*. Most don't like saying the system is corrupt. Saying it out loud is too dispiriting. But if you watch what people do, in contrast to what they say, their actions bespeak their truths. People act as if boss pleasing is a totally essential criterion for pay enhancements, good job assignments, and career progress. They behave as if every aspect of their job, including their future in the company, significantly depends on satisfying their boss's ego. They behave as if significant setbacks and penalties will be levied for expressing even minor disagreement and voicing alternative points of view. Fearing the worst, they go overboard, stating and restating what they believe the boss wants to hear, as if each exchange were an impromptu loyalty test.

Bosses and people in superior positions extend this corruption in two interrelated ways. First, they enter a state of denial, acting as if the buttered-up treatment rendered them by lowers were genuine and deserved. They forget the distrust they feel as subordinates interacting with their superiors. They overlook the deception they use to create the impression of agreement and harmony. They earnestly believe lowers have nothing to fear from saying things straight, exactly as they see them. Second, uppers fear having their performance diminished by actions of a lower they were supposed to direct and control. Aggressively, they distance themselves from failed efforts and subordinates' miscues by blaming and faulting the very subordinates they selected, whose effectiveness it was their job to ensure. They may give lip service to work unit teamwork, but their critical commentaries are aimed at catapulting blame downward.

Recognizing these dynamics, subordinates shamelessly spend hours preparing project and program reviews that say what their bosses want to hear and accomplish what they think their boss wants to achieve, oftentimes in a format that conceals how they honestly see the situation and what they actually think. In our experience, it's a rare day when a subordinate tells it straight without undue concern for what he or she thinks a "superior" will tolerate; and it is yet a rarer day when a superior will stand accountable for his or her role in a subordinate's failed effort.

IF YOU OWNED THE ENTERPRISE, WHAT WOULD YOU SAY WAS WRONG?

If you owned a company and could not be on site to perform surveillance, you would be bothered by a management system that allowed top-level people to hold mid- and lower-level people accountable without these people being able to raise questions about what they saw wrong or out of whack. You'd be upset because you'd know that everyone has limited perspective, especially on matters that impact one's image and bear on criteria used in measuring job success. You'd know that everyone makes mistakes and would be uncomfortable about having a system that allows any individual's mistakes to go undetected or covered-up. You would desire honest give-and-take communication as a process that protects your assets when you aren't around.

Your concerns would be heightened if you thought lowers believed the criteria used to evaluate their performance included catering to their boss's ego and placing their boss's interests ahead of what they see as best for the company. Instantly, you would think the system corrupt and begin looking for a better one. But you would be hard-pressed to specify a better way of operating that didn't anger bosses who want you to see their management practices as fair-minded and to think that their doors are always open to subordinates who want dialogue. As owner you would want to hold your top-level people accountable for engaging divergent viewpoints but would find it difficult to specify a plan.

In the absence of such a plan, you'd probably do what we see most corporate-level executives do: cultivate networks of informants and spies. You'd find opportunities to ask mid- and lower-level employees, especially those you've known for years, "How is it *really* going?" and generally pump them for information bearing on operational issues and management. You'd find informed individuals to take to lunch for "friendly conversation" and with whom to bum rides to the airport. You'd help friends and relatives get jobs in the company and then make sure they kept you abreast of company activities. Creatively, you'd exploit almost any interaction as an opportunity to check what's "actually" going on.

Initially mid- and lower-level people are unaware of being used as spies, but eventually they figure it out. Once they do so, they often self-corrupt. Their natural, only somewhat self-interested, accounts are replaced with politically calculated versions. And because the spying function they perform is surreptitious, the only system for ensuring objectivity available to the executives using this method of surveillance is to broaden their network of spies. They clandestinely install a system of faulty *two-sided accountability* that ultimately is no more objective than the one-sided accountability system their management has in place.[1]

THE CORE PROBLEM IS ONE-SIDED ACCOUNTABILITY!

To put it in a nutshell, the problem with hierarchical relationships is *one-sided accountability*. Uppers get to evaluate lowers without a system that ensures evaluation fairness or reciprocal critique. As a system, one-sided accountability blocks straightforward, honest, "tell it how you see it" communication. It's a system that prevents messages from registering even when, for whatever extraordinary reason, you've got a subordinate who wants to tell it straight. One-sided accountability prevented the executive who checked up on

---

[1]What's happening here is the same process we criticize when someone suggests a 360-degree feedback. People self-corrupt: they figure out what evaluations and judgments feed their personal interests and then provide a calculated response.

our buddy from telling it straight to his CEO boss. It prevented the Human Resources person who ambushed us after class from getting engagement for a message he repeatedly sent. And it was the cause of angst and frustration for a manager we're about to describe who felt blocked in saving his company millions of dollars. As you read on, consider the frustrations he experienced trying to extract responsible behavior from a boss who could hide from him using the one-sided accountability cloak of an obviously hierarchical relationship.

Statement of One-Sided Accountability

> My boss is totally hierarchical in his thinking. Whenever I bring up an issue he doesn't want to discuss, he likes to say, "Sounds like you have a problem." Then he says, "You don't have to bother me; just go out and fix it and tell me what you've done." If I persist, saying, "I'd like a little discussion," he reiterates, "It's your problem; just fix it." This places me in a position where my only safe course is to give him the fix he expects. That way I save myself the humiliation of listening to him ask, "Why didn't you do this or that?" the way he thinks is right. So while I learned not to bring him problems, I still have to get his agreement to chase an opportunity. Unfortunately, it's almost impossible to get any focus for an issue that isn't on his screen. In fact, just last week his unwillingness to engage me cost the company over a million dollars, and I've got the hard facts to document this. It would have been a quick "buy-sell" with no transaction costs."

One-Side-Accountable Command-and-Control Exists in All Hierarchical Relationships, Even When It's Difficult to Spot

When accountability is one-sided, inevitably politics supercede the truth. Of course, as every pundit knows, the best political strategy is truth telling. But, as we've explored elsewhere,[2] even telling the truth

---

[2]Samuel A. Culbert and John J. McDonough, *The Invisible War: Pursuing Self-Interests at Work* (New York: Wiley, 1980).

as you actually believe it does not rule out duplicity, self-justified spin, and information rationing. In the end, the result is inevitable. It's one-side-accountable ***command-and-control***, even when you can't see it. In fact, if one-sided accountability were a right hook, we'd all be lying on the canvas knocked out cold. It's the sucker punch that catches us with our guards down.

For an example of the invisibility of one-sided accountability consider the plum assignment an up-and-coming young professional received when a positively intentioned boss decided to do her a favor. See if you can spot the command-and-control. Most people miss it so we'll give you a big hint. It's right in front of your eyes, folded in with what the boss related. Here's how the boss told it to us.

SHORT CASE

The MBA Who Wants to Star

"I've got this extremely bright MBA who has been champing at the bit for an opportunity to show her 'stuff.' Along comes a request for us to streamline our unit. So to give her some visibility, I ask her to formulate our plan. I tell her, 'Feel free to consult with our guys and to interview suppliers, customers, and those in the company who interact with us.' Then I tell her, 'When you're through, put your recommendations in writing and we'll take them to my boss.'"

Ever on the alert for hidden command-and-control, we inquired, "Are you and your boss on her list of people to interview?" When he answered, "No," we knew the outcome. We thought, "Another KO by sucker punch." Then, merely to establish a data point for subsequent conversation, we asked, "Why isn't she interviewing the two of you?" He responded, "We're sincerely undecided about how to reorganize, and we didn't want our viewpoints to be overly influential."

If ever a work assignment had locked in command-and-control, this one did. We felt bad that this time a self-professed good guy, a boss who takes pride in mentoring young professionals, was the initiating agent. Worse yet, command-and-control was never his intention. Along with the bright MBA recipient, he missed seeing the dynamics he had initiated.

Precisely what did he miss? Where did we see command-and-control?

We saw command-and-control the moment we reflected on what it would take for this MBA to discuss her data and conclusions on a level playing field with two tiers of her bosses. In addition to coming up with a viable solution, she would be thinking about the impression she was making and what it would mean for her career with the company. Given the stakes, we were concerned that not knowing the bosses' thoughts and assumptions going in would set her up for hierarchical intimidation.

Only by interviewing the bosses prior to formulating her conclusions could she achieve the measure of two-sided accountability needed for holding a give-and-take discussion with viewpoint parity. Knowing their views at the beginning, she would have had time to place them in the context of what she was learning and thinking about with others. This would also have given her time to formulate her reorganizational schema and to prepare an ego-sensitive framing of conclusions that differed with her bosses' initial thinking. She might even have begun her presentation with an overview and critique of their viewpoints. Then, with their logic exposed, she might have used the data she collected to take them to the next level.

Knowing the bosses' viewpoints prior to concluding her analysis contrasts dramatically with not knowing those viewpoints yet having them act as the back-of-the-mind standards her bosses used when contemplating the validity of her conclusions. This is where presenters get "yes, butted" into submission. Gradually she would get exposed to their viewpoints, but the process would be painful. She'd encounter their thoughts and opinions in questions like, "Yes, but have you considered this?" "Yes, but how do you deal with the concern raised in last week's executive briefing you didn't attend?" Scenarios like this are common in hierarchical relationships. And all parties lose when they're played out. Bosses are disappointed, subordinates are shamed, and the company fails to benefit from human resources paid for and expended.

Bosses use one-sided accountability to get subordinates to do things their way, to attend worthless meetings they feel forced to say are valuable, and to withhold point-of-view differences that are front and center on their minds. One-sided accountability allows bosses to continuously ask, "What have you done for me lately?" without facing the complementary question of their subordinates, "How are you helping me produce what we both agreed the company needs from me which, admittedly, I haven't accomplished?"

At this point we'd like to call your attention to Table A, which displays some characteristic consequences of hierarchical relationships. We intend it as a prompt for thinking about the missed opportunities and losses in organizational productivity associated with hierarchical relationships. This table also suggests what people in boss and subordinate roles, or in nonparity power situations, have to gain by changing the one-sided accountability assumption built into their relationships.

TWO-SIDED ACCOUNTABILITY IS REQUIRED!

All of the cases presented so far depict organizationally destructive dynamics set in play due to subordinates in hierarchical relationships being unable to extract a measure of reciprocal accountability from those to whom they report. In fact, we believe each instance of organizational ineffectiveness would have dissipated if the upper-level person was also accountable. In every situation we believe the remedy would have been a two-sides-accountable relationship. Of course, what a person might be held accountable for differs by hierarchical role, functional responsibilities, and organizational structure.

To review, the Rampart panel's framing of the LAPD case appeared to hold no one beyond first-level supervisors accountable for monitoring officer conduct and creating the conditions for officers to perform their jobs properly and effectively. If people at each successive level were to be held directly accountable for the conduct and effectiveness of cops, how could they find out what accepting that accountability entails? Simple, all they'd need is a list of troublesome incidents, statistics, and candid dialoguing with the people directly above and below them. Then they would know. But even hearing this would require stepping out of the pass-the-buck mentality that causes them to fear that any acknowledged deficiency in the way they have been operating would be used to "ding" them for actions not previously taken.

And what about the CEO in our case "Who Performed the Most Outrageous Act?"? He's the one who failed to learn about his pattern of organizationally disruptive self-indulgence, because his subordinate executive, with data in hand, seemed afraid to tell him. We think he would have been told if he were accountable for providing his direct reports the sense of well-being that they require to candidly interact with him. "The Boss Who Wouldn't Deliver Needed Help" case depicts a boss who wasn't even accountable for an unwillingness to communicate, this time with an operation in crisis waiting for authorization to hire more resources. Likewise with the boss whose subordinate complained "his unwillingness to communicate just cost the company a million dollars." And the MBA graduate who wanted to "star" wasn't going to do so without her bosses' sharing their going-in assumptions and opinions that, in the context of their hierarchical relationships, she lacked the means for insisting they provide.

CONTRASTING ONE-SIDED AND TWO-SIDED ACCOUNTABILITY

In a one-side-accountable, hierarchical relationship, the boss, or party with the power advantage, holds the subordinate, or party with less power, accountable for delivering certain results. The boss may even utilize his or her hierarchical authority to stipulate

	TABLE A RESULTS OF ONE-SIDE-ACCOUNTABLE, HIERARCHICAL RELATIONSHIPS
Teamwork	**Illusionary Teamwork** *Bosses and subordinates alike tend to* break team activities into component elements with each person taking care not to intrude into a domain assigned to someone else. People take steps to ensure that others see them pulling their weight and performing competently. *Bosses* fail to create the conditions for give-and-take interaction, risk taking, and people getting actively involved in a function or responsibility assigned to someone else. *Subordinates* take care to appear cooperative while seeing themselves competing for pay, plum assignments, and promotion.
Communication	**Warped Communication** *Bosses and subordinates alike tend to* shape and tailor their communications with emphasis on framing events and telling versions of the truth in ways that fit their self-interests. *Bosses* operate with command-and-control reasoning but take care to give the impression that they are even-handed, fair-minded, and ever open to new ideas. *Subordinates* withhold viewpoints and perceptions that they see conflicting with those held by a boss. They seek to portray themselves as loyal, capable, energetic contributors.
Internal Politics	**Corrupt Internal Politics** *Bosses and subordinates alike tend to* practice win-win politics as usual. The first win is what's good for one's self, the second what's good for the company. In practice, the first win is dominant but hidden. *Bosses* expect subordinates to meet performance goals without considering how the means to achieving them aligns with the subordinate's interests. *Subordinates* form idea coalitions with people they see as possessing the power either to do them some good or, if provoked, to hurt them.
Accountability	**Pass-the-Buck Accountability** *Bosses and subordinates alike tend to* practice "accountability avoidance," stationing themselves to elude blame for actions taken or withheld. *Bosses* use directives and performance reviews to coerce subordinates to accomplish what they want done. *Subordinates* feel vulnerable and defensively take care to perform as stipulated and directed. They justify their actions on the "input" grounds of properly performing as instructed.
Morale	**Personal Dispiriting** *Bosses and subordinates alike tend to* miss the overlap in one another's motives, often experiencing one another as adversaries. *Bosses* believe subordinates lack motivation and need prodding to communicate or take initiative. *Subordinates* spend time planning how to communicate ideas that uppers will find acceptable. They are frustrated by having to perform work they believe is misdirected and wasteful of their time and scarce company resources, with no avenue open for discussing their actual beliefs and perceptions.

TABLE B   RESULTS OF TWO-SIDES-ACCOUNTABLE RELATIONSHIPS

Teamwork

Authentic Teamwork

Bosses and subordinates alike tend to see looking out for teammate and company interests as also good for themselves. They see giving and receiving of teammate assistance as essential to a successful effort.

Bosses take responsibility for ensuring that relevant "voices" are heard and contrasting viewpoints discussed. They credit people for actions that assist others to address and accomplish team goals.

Subordinates put energy into tracking team progress and feel responsible for picking up the slack and insinuating themselves when they believe someone on the team needs help.

Communication

Straight-Talk Communication

Bosses and subordinate alike tend to tell the truth as they know it and seek the truth as the other person knows it.

Bosses surface disagreements and facilitate expressive and open discussions prior to taking action. They provide reasons for decisions made and make sure that subordinates with divergent views feel sufficiently valued to express those views.

Subordinates attempt candor in expressing divergent viewpoints. When they fear that a divergent view will be held against them, they enlist assistance from others.

Internal Politics

Aboveboard Politics

Bosses and subordinates alike tend to practice win-win-win politics—they seek a win for themselves, a win for the company, and a win for other relevant parties. They reason that the corporate endeavor advances when others are fully contributing and functioning at peak effectiveness.

Bosses seek out divergent perspectives to see if they are overlooking something essential, knowing that people up and down the chain will be looking at results to hold them accountable.

Subordinates are responsive to the boss's interests knowing that their own have been heard out. They keep focused on goals the boss sets forth while doing what they think best for themselves and the company in achieving them.

Accountability

Stand-and-Be-Counted Accountability

Bosses and subordinates alike tend to stand accountable for the total effort as well as their individual functions and roles.

Bosses put considerable effort into producing a clearly articulated organization chart that assigns people with responsibility the authority to exercise it, providing others the means to hold people with responsibility accountable for results. They encourage subordinates to learn about one another's competencies, limitations, and life situations and provide a context that justifies someone pitching in as needs to do so are spotted.

Subordinates keep abreast of how others are performing to ascertain whether their input is required. Reciprocally, they open themselves to receiving assistance when others think it's needed.

Morale

Esprit de Corps

Bosses and subordinates alike tend to position themselves to do their best, seeing the roles they play as reciprocally beneficial. They are positive in their reactions to setback, believing that the conditions for them to excel are still in place.

Bosses operate on the assumption that subordinates want to do well. They assume an active role staging for their subordinates' success.

Subordinates feel invigorated expressing their ideas knowing that others are listening. They seek to learn from different viewpoints knowing that ultimately their evaluation will be based on actual outcomes and performance results.

means, time frame, and methodology, as well as the criteria used in measuring success. Who is boss, and the basis of that person's authority, are determined by the organization chart.

A two-sides-accountable relationship cedes most of the same to the boss but goes a step further by holding the boss accountable for taking actions that facilitate the subordinate's success. It connects the boss to the results with such immutability that finger pointing begins with oneself. The question at hand changes from "Why didn't you perform competently the way I directed?" to "How do you see it? What background, coaching, support, and assistance do you need from me?" Faced with the former, people confabulate; faced with the latter, their inclination is to tell it straight. They explain what they need but aren't getting, and they candidly report what they think and see.

By holding bosses accountable, two-sided accountability inverts hierarchical structure, providing the people directing work a need to communicate openly and accurately with those performing it. This has always been what organizations need; there's nothing new about it. But caught in the hierarchy trap, people systematically slip up.

The next chapters explain the transformations required for negotiating the change from a hierarchical to a two-sides-accountable mind-set. Table B serves as a means of contrasting the changes required and behavioral benefits received, and as a road map of issues and benefits soon to be discussed.

SUMMARY

In this chapter we've pinpointed the toxic element in hierarchical relationships as one-sided accountability. We've characterized the predictable negative outcomes as warped communication, corrupt internal politics, illusionary teamwork, pass-the-buck accountability, and personal dispiriting. We've identified the methodology as command-and-control management and one-sided accountability intimidation. But we haven't identified why these blatantly awful situations are allowed to exist and proliferate. That topic begins in the next chapter.

3

Transformation 1

You've Got to Use What You Know
about Human Nature

Chapters 1 and 2 depict *two-sided accountability* as the positive alternative to hierarchical relationships, as the thinking that can release you and your company from the hierarchy trap. If two-sided accountability is the solution, then why isn't it more familiar? Why hasn't an epidemic of two-sides-accountable relationships swept through the corporate world, setting the stage for *straight-talk communication*, *aboveboard politics*, *authentic teamwork*, *esprit de corps*, and *stand-and-be-counted accountability*?

We think two-sided accountability would be mainstream if adding some goodwill commitments to balance the boss's side of the boss/subordinate "accountability equation" were all that was required. But that's not how it works. While the term *two-sided accountability* implies reciprocity, precisely which accountabilities constitute reciprocity differ by level, function, structure, and role. They can only be determined after seeing what a specific subordinate, with unique talents, limitations and life quests, and with commitments you could never predict, faces in succeeding in a specific assignment.

Making accountability reciprocal requires two significant transformations, each necessitating changes in mind-set and actions. The first transformation entails facing up to basic human nature facts regarding the always present subjective and self-interested framework people impose on their experiences at work, and then applying this understanding to one's everyday dealings with others. The second entails facing up to the inherently political dimension that characterizes all workplace interactions and learning how to conduct those politics aboveboard with a team-playing orientation. Only by ignoring these facts can people proceed as if they can form hierarchical relationships without significant negatives to themselves and the company.

FALSE OBJECTIVITY IS A HURDLE TO OVERCOME

This chapter deals with the first transformational topic: the inherently subjective nature of people's experiences at work and the *false objectivity* people hide behind in concealing their self-interests. Pretending that people ought to be objective necessitates putting people into categories. You can't say what people want or how they should act or what motivates them without thinking categorically. But we don't know anyone who considers him- or herself to be a lockstep member of a category. We can't ever recall an executive who accepted being lumped into any category or behavioral dimension with other executives. And for years we've watched students flinch in apparent discomfort whenever they thought they were being put in the category of "all MBAs" with equivalent attributions regarding abilities, needs, motivations, or sociology.

To the contrary, all work experiences are subjectively felt and self-interestedly interpreted. Each individual's reaction is entirely personal. This is not to say that people don't attempt objectivity by overriding their immediate reactions with intellect or possess zones of sensitivity and vulnerability that make them so anxious that they appear to act without consciousness of what they are experiencing viscerally. We're merely asserting that everyone reacts psychologically, and, conscious of doing so or not, intellect is applied after emotion. Thus, regardless of the false objectivity people use in portraying work events and rationalizing their reactions on the basis of what is objectively required of them, what people experience and how they act or react is far more subjective and self-interested than it is objective and company-focused.

For this discussion we've decided to invoke the dialogical method we often use to ignite emotions when teaching in the executive classroom. Without emotional involvement, your head goes away with the knowledge but your behavior remains the same. It's not just a matter of learning the principles and facts that will enable you to escape the hierarchy trap. It's a matter of shifting your logic. We're talking about adjusting the paradigm you use, not specific steps you must take. We're working on the belief that when you think differently, you'll never be comfortable in a hierarchical relationship again.

To start the process, we begin where we left off in Chapter 2, painting a picture of people stuck in unproductive hierarchical relationships. Now we ask you, "What makes them so stuck?" Given the problems associated with hierarchical relationships, why haven't people smartened up? Why do they persist in forming the types of relationships that inevitably become losing propositions for themselves and the company? The short answer implied by the title of this chapter is that they haven't found a way to put what they *almost* know about human nature to use. As you'll see in the chapter's concluding discussion, putting it to use is a must for resisting one-side-accountable, hierarchical relationships.

Years of teaching, consulting, and research have led us to conclude that most people aren't paying sufficient attention to what they already realize and know. How do we know this? Because if they had internalized some basic principles, they would have long ago recognized the futility of their attachments to hierarchy and gone all out finding other ways to relate. In making this indictment we include bosses and subordinates alike, even professionals who consider themselves "people persons."

It's ironic, since most people recognize the overlooked facts to the extent that just as soon as we list them on the board, they begin volunteering personal experiences that attest to their validity. But until we confront them with the inadequacy of their responses to elementary questions about work and daily living, people seem unable to accept that what their heads know bears little on every-day actions. This leaves us believing that until some significant oversight touches them emotionally, their head-level knowledge will continue to be insufficient to dislodge their default-setting proclivity for hierarchical relationships.

WE INVITE YOU TO JOIN THE CLASS

To illustrate these principles and how we struggle in getting people to put them into action, we want to expose you to the questions we use in our own attempts to help people break their hierarchical relationship proclivities. We want to touch them personally and emotionally. As we raise these questions, try answering them your-self. In fact, jot down what you would actually think, say, and do. Afterward continue reading to see how your answers compare with the ones we've received from managers and executives taking an *opening exam* in a ten-session course entitled "Leadership, Motivation, and Power" and the our answers we later provide.

The first question is **"What's the second thing you should say to someone who tells you 'I just received a promotion?'"** Of course, the first thing you'll probably say is "Congratulations." Social protocol dictates this response. But what's the second thing?

The second question is **"If the sign says, 'Street Cleaning— No Parking 10 A.M. until Noon,' and the street cleaner comes by at 10:30, will you get a ticket if you park there fifteen min- utes later at 10:45?"**

The third question refers to a situation that everyone in a management position repeatedly experiences, which should make answering it easy. **"Let's say you want to give an assignment, one that you can state clearly and with some degree of preci- sion. What's the best way to communicate the assignment to the person you are asking to perform it?"**

Take a few minutes to answer these questions before reading on.

We find that most people are overly generous in excusing the errors they make when answering commonsense questions they believe they *ought* to be able to answer correctly. In the case of our audience, this tendency impedes their learning the very thing we most want them to know—that there's incoherence in their thinking about people. To combat this *generosity* and to maximize the chances that our audience will take their test results seriously, we go through the motions of making our questions appear to be a serious exam. We ask people to write their names on the top of a blank piece of paper, instruct them to work independently, and then collect their papers prior to going over their answers.

When answering the first question, "What's the second thing to say to someone after hearing of that person's promotion?" most people give a political response. They state variations of "That's great—you really deserved it," and "Let me know if ever I can be of help." Few who would make such self-ingratiating remarks realize what they are up to so we make it a point to needle them good-naturedly. Thumbing through the "exams" we've collected, we shake our heads in mock disgust. Waiting a moment to make it dramatic, we put on a wry smile and wisecrack, "Oh, no! Not another politically motivated, kiss-up response!" This is our attempt to induce a measure of frustration before giving them an obvious answer that most could not, given the way they actually think about people and operate, come up with on their own.

The answer we give is actually a question: "Tell me, what does this promotion mean to you?" We explain, "We all know everyone is different, has a unique life situation, and possesses distinctive personal resources, which means that you can't guess the meaning a situation holds for another individual merely by thinking about the meaning it would hold for you. You have to ask the individual. For example, a technical task force leader who was promoted to business unit leader, a position that, in a profitable year, could easily double his pay, responded with great ambivalence. He said, 'I don't think managing people runs in my family genes. In fact, last year my pharmacist sister was promoted to managing the pharmacy, and after performing successfully for six months asked to return to filling prescriptions. Like her, I'm a hands-on operator. I much prefer the challenge of solving high-tech problems to administration and managing people.'"

For emphasis, we next engage in some lighthearted chiding. We want our students to comprehend the significance of their answers being *graded wrong*. Scratching our heads, we inquire, "How come you're not seriously bothered by your wrong answer?" Here we're looking to get someone to own up and tell us what we suspect a preponderance of people think. Almost always we can get someone to say, "I'm not that bothered because actually I already knew this." That is our setup to reemphasize our main point, one that readily gets lost in the specifics, "Please tell us why you didn't state what you already know?" We seek to confront people with the illogical point that knowing the right answer was their excuse for not using it. It's a confrontation we attempt to continue reviewing responses to the second question.

People typically answer the second question—whether or not they would get a ticket—with a yes. We press them to explain the basis for their conclusion. Elaborating, they portray ticket writers as categorically unthinking and unfeeling individuals with quotas to fill, who mindlessly go by the "book."

Then we give our answer, which is "It depends on the mindset of the ticket writer." We explain that there's no way of knowing how a particular ticket writer thinks, and we like to think that some are like each of the people in our class, desirous of placing function over form, and would resist writing a ticket. We tell them that we've questioned many ticket writers, and every one has given at least lip service to being a function oriented person who would see no point in writing a ticket.

It is interesting to note that the answers people give to the third question—the best way to give an assignment—are not that different from the ones our consulting clients give when we ask what's the best way. Typical of the answers we receive are "I make sure to state the assignment clearly, draw the connection between it and overarching company goals, and conclude with 'Do you have any questions?'" "I describe the career expanding opportunities it holds and how the assignment will allow the individual to demonstrate his or her effectiveness." "I make sure to emphasize the due date and my willingness to help twenty-four hours a day, seven days a week." People state the ideal to the point where we get the impression that much of what we're hearing isn't completely true. In some instances, a surreptitious checking up has caught a person telling a lie. For example, in response to our question a senior VP of a company listed on the New York Stock Exchange made a point of looking us in the eye when he said, "After I give an assignment, I always write it down and give a copy to the individual." Later, in response to our off-the-cuff inquiry, his secretary laughingly told us, "You must be talking about a different Jeff. The guy I work for has never written anything down and issues convoluted decrees, not clearly formulated instructions."

We think our answer is far more practical, and it often takes people by surprise. We say, "Give the assignment any way you want; no doubt you are experienced and have evolved your own way of saying things effectively. But, after waiting a few days, we advise you to drop by the recipient's office for an informal visit to casually inquire, 'How are things going? What's on your mind?' 'What's your number one priority?' 'What other projects concern you?' 'What's your current thinking, and when do you think you can get to the project I recently asked you to handle?' 'What's likely to be your time frame?' 'How are you fixed for budget and resources?' 'Are you going to need my help?' And so on."

Giving this advice we emphasize that they should low-key their questions and focus intensively on what they hear. We tell them that this Columbo-type inquiry is likely to provide their last true look at how the other person sees the project and what they need to be aware of in getting desired results. We explain that the value of this inquiry is diagnosis, not control, and that an assignment giver needs a valid picture of what he or she is likely to receive prior to reasserting missing priorities and reemphasizing methodology. We tell them, "Only after you know what was omitted, misinterpreted, and differently prioritized will you know what you actually need to do to get the results you want."

Throughout this exercise, our mission is less to give people the right answers and more to confront them with the fact that their answers to these rather elementary and practical questions weren't very good. We want them to entertain the idea that they might be operating with an inferior paradigm.

Now it's time for us to introduce the critical paradigm, the one that relies on what people already know about human nature but is systematically overlooked in the responses they made to the three practical questions we posed. In introducing this paradigm, we explain the underlying reasons for the questions we chose. We tell people, "The first question bears on the issue of diversity and the fact that every individual is different to the point that understanding an individual's mind-set is an essential prerequisite for comprehending the meaning of his or her words." Elaborating, we say, "Different people take the same action for different reasons. To know what an individual is up to, you have to ask what he or she is doing and why the person thinks it necessary."

The second question elaborates the paradigm. In going back over the question, we tell our audience that the "Yes, you'll get a ticket" answer is the old "Uptight Human Resources won't allow it" response. It's the response of individuals who, frustrated by past experiences, have stereotyped the entire Human Resource department as unnecessarily bureaucratic and gutless in taking actions that deviate from what line managers want and what HR has stated is "going by the book." These are individuals who feel they have been turned down by procedure, not reason.

This question provides us the opportunity to assert that treating any group or unit as a category is a self-defeating action that shuts the door on originality and creativity and causes worst-case scenarios to come true. We tell our audience, "There is no Human Resource department. There are merely unique individuals who work in the human resources discipline who, regardless of the treatment you've experienced to date, may be willing to help you out." When you find an individual citing a procedure that blocks you, you need to engage that individual. You need to get that person thinking about your plan for being effective and his or her role in helping you do what's needed. If that person agrees but tells you "My hands are tied," then the problem is his or her hierarchy. Now it's time to switch tracks to help that individual with his or her problem so that he or she can then do what's right for you. We allege, "There is no organization outside of the minds of the people who view it." We urge people to always ask those they see blocking them questions aimed at clarifying their underlying thinking.

The third, "how do you give an assignment" question provides an opportunity to anchor the audience in our paradigm. Starkly, we tell them, "Communication is a tricky phenomenon. If you want to know what you said, find out what the other person heard." We explain, "Stop acting as if work life shouldn't be political. People with different agendas and different personal resources will always impute different meanings to events. What could be more natural!" We then tell them, "Organization life is inherently political," and we define politics as the dynamics created by people with different self-interested needs arguing about what is required for the organization or company to succeed. We explain that, in most instances, "people honestly see events the way they portray them, which nearly always includes a rationale that casts outcomes that are good for them as outcomes that are good for the company. What's more problematic," we explain, "is whether the other person's self-interested framing of events is sufficiently valid for you." We caution, "You waste valuable time worrying whether the self-serving and self-convenient framing of events expressed by others is correct and moral when the real issue is to get the other person to include your high-priority interests in with the way he or she frames things." Getting back to the question, we tell the audience, "If you want to find out what another individual is actually doing and why that person thinks it needs to be done, you need to ask questions—lots of them!"

People almost always agree with these points, and many cite their own experiences to support them. But getting people to acknowledge these truths of human nature is not the same as getting people to internalize them. For this we have another ploy.

We begin the next session pretending that we have graded the turned-in papers and that the grades fall somewhere between failing and abysmal. Talk about deference to hierarchy—some people begin to act as if our bogus grade counted. We ask our audience once again to take out a piece of paper, write down their name, and answer one more question that, if answered correctly, will cancel out a bad grade. Not sure how to read us, people dutifully go along. For us this is a crescendo opportunity to pose them the home run question. We ask, "What is it you didn't know, or you knew but could not find a way of articulating on last week's exam, that prevented you from more accurately answering the three questions?" Then we watch their tortured expressions as once again their brains search for an answer they think they ought to know.

Despite the pains we take to sound tough, our softheartedness gets in the way. Instead of allowing people the agony of trying to get it themselves, we quickly slip them the aspirin. In response to their grimacing faces, we lower the projection screen and flash on a slide that says, "Organization is an artifact of the mind that views it."

This slogan[1] is our way of explaining that the reality an individual experiences at work is, in every instance, a unique and self-manufactured one. Citing the old 1940s experiment,[2] we tell them, "Researchers who asked children to draw pictures of coins flashed on a screen found that kids from poorer families drew high-denomination coins larger than their well-to-do counterparts drew them." We then emphasize that, likewise, managers, leaders, and executives make a critical error whenever they act as if they can

---

[1]The expression "Organization is an artifact of the mind that views it" is explored extensively in S. A. Culbert, *Mind-Set Management: The Heart of Leadership* (New York: Oxford University Press, 1996).

[2]J. S. Bruner and C. C. Goldman. "Value and Need as Organizing Factors in Perception," *Journal of Abnormal and Social Psychology* 42 (1947): 33–44.

accurately predict how someone will react or accurately interpret the meaning of someone's behavior without first understanding that person's motivation, perspective, background, and viewpoint.

Discussing the meaning of "Organization is an artifact of the mind that views it," we find that most people only understand part. Quickly they pick up on the point that others interpret events idiosyncratically. Instrumentally they resolve, probably for the umpteenth time in their lives, to be sure to ask how the people with whom they work see events and problems prior to drawing conclusions. The part they don't immediately process, and which we gently extract from them, is that they, too, organize organizational happenings in self-interested and biased ways. We push this point until we can get everyone to chant "I am a biased viewer. My self-interested needs are encased in everything I see, say, and do."

Basic as this point is, some people fight it. We find that having it out with individuals who insist that their views are objective creates important instructional moments, less for them and more for the onlookers. We seize these moments in an effort to hammer the last nail in the coffin of their rational management mind-sets.

Missing the self-interested side of the "artifact of mind," inevitable subjectivity axiom leads to at least three important human interaction mistakes. First, until authentically grasped and internalized, an individual misses the fact that human imperfection and self-interested bias are present in every situation and that what he or she is inclined to call the organization's "objective reality" is always a subjectively motivated characterization. It is determined by some individual's or group's or company's self-interested depiction of what is or should be taking place.

Second, unless the principle of self-interested viewpoints and constant bias is internalized, people miss obvious and important opportunities to comprehend what personalized assumptions are contained in someone else's assessment of what's taking place and to inquire into its basis. This is why they fail to ask, "How do you see it? Why do you see it that way?"

Third, people who have not internalized these principles are inclined to take the moral high ground. They justify self-serving, standard-breaking, interpersonally competitive actions on the grounds that they are necessary for serving a higher-order organizational cause without identifying what's self-convenient for themselves.

CHANGING THE PARADIGM

The dialogical process we invoke was selected for its ability to stimulate self-reflection and vicarious learning. It is aimed at provoking people to replay past experiences to see how their efforts to create a "rational" world have caused them to project their self-interested motives on others, put others in false categories, and objectify others by neglecting their subjectively based, self-interested pursuits. In essence, we are attempting to motivate our audience to replace their paradigm of false objectivity with a rekindled and self-enlightened appreciation for "the artifact of mind" theory of *inevitable subjectivity*.

Continuing our explanation, we posit that everyone comes to work with a single motivation, which is to live his or her *total life* competently. We say a great deal about this, but for our purposes here we emphasize that there is much more behind what a person does at work than any logically derived explanation of his or her work behavior alone can reveal. The fact that another person may seldom or never act as you think he or she should in response to organizational needs as you see them does not mean the person is only screwing up. His or her seemingly incompetent behavior might very well serve some higher-order personal priority. After all, we explain, you can't expect an individual not to speed and run a red light while taking a child with an emergency to the hospital.

IMPLICATIONS FOR HIERARCHICAL RELATIONSHIPS

We characterize hierarchical relationships as corrupting and illusion generating and believe that such relationships always cost the company, whether or not they benefit either or both of the participants.

We empathetically acknowledge the pressures a lower-level person feels to tilt the truth toward what he or she believes the upper-level person wants to hear. We bemoan the problems that beset upper-level people who, in not receiving a balanced picture, misconstrue and get an inflated view of their personal intelligence and the correctness of what they believe. We decry the consequences.

The negatives of hierarchical relationships are immediately discernible for the individual operating with an internalized "Organization is an artifact of the mind that views it" mind-set. That person knows each individual views events uniquely, according to his or her self-interests, ambitions, and self-perceived competencies. That person accepts the inevitability of bias; acknowledges that he or she, like everyone else, functions with self-interests; and understands that all organizational decisions must be practically plausible in light of the needs, perceptions, and competencies of the people expected to carry them out, or distortion will follow.

WE TAKE THE TEST

To see how we're doing in getting an audience to internalize these lessons, we conduct another spot exam. Explaining that the exam question emanates from a real time consultation, we pose the following problem: "Assume you're in a meeting with six of your organizational peers, none of whom you see as high-intelligence Menses material. Discussing an important matter, someone makes a suggestion that you are absolutely sure will take the group in the wrong direction. Immediately you see two choices: either set her straight and risk the consequences of being seen as not really interested in other people's thinking, or grin and bear it, allowing the group to waste valuable time, energy, and group spirit. Can you think of a third alternative? In any event, state your choice and what you are inclined to say or do. Jot down some notes. This time we'll make it a group quiz."

What we don't tell people at the time, and what they probably don't recognize but is on our mind when raising this question, is that the two alternatives alluded to in our question are both hierarchical relationship responses. Asking people to think of a third alternative is offering them the opportunity to come up with a nonhierarchical response.

After giving them time to contemplate their answers, we begin the discussion by asking "Which of you plan to give a 'third alternative' answer?" This time we're looking to validate, not disconfirm. We're looking for people who can use "tell me what it means to you," *inevitable subjectivity* thinking to acknowledge a difference in opinion in a relationship-building, supportive way. In this specific context, it's some variation of "This is interesting—I'm so different in my thinking that I can't follow your response. Help me. Tell me how you've got our situation framed and the problem you are solving by the way you think we should proceed. Show me how your proposal fits with how you see things." Of course, no one uses these exact words.

CONCLUSION

We're after recognition of two basic facts of human nature which, when internalized, support two-sided accountability thinking. The first: **You must never count on anyone seeing or experiencing an event exactly as you see and experience it.** The second: **You cannot evaluate the sensibility of someone else's suggestion for proceeding until you comprehend the logic underlying it.** When these facts are internally accepted, not just spoken, all organizational events are approached differently. Bosses stop assuming that subordinates see events as they see them and experience the need to go beyond a nodding head to get to the basis of the other person's thinking. Subordinates go beyond stereotyping boss spoken directives. They probe the basis of a boss's thinking to determine the extent to which give-and-take, interactive discussion is possible. A summary of how this mind-set contrasts with the one used in hierarchical relationships is included in Table C.

TABLE C CONTRASTING MIND-SETS: HUMAN NATURE	
One-Side-Accountable, Hierarchical Relationships	**Two-Sides-Accountable Relationships**
False Objectivity	**Inevitable Subjectivity**
Bosses and subordinates alike place people in categories with standard expectations for all members of that category. *Bosses* underestimate the value of candid subordinate input and over-estimate the comprehensiveness and accuracy of their own views. *Subordinates* grouse about differing viewpoints with the boss and are quick to attribute them to boss shortsightedness and disorientation.	*Bosses and subordinates alike* assume each individual views events uniquely, according to his or her self-interests, ambitions, and self-perceived competencies. Both accept that personal considerations as well as functionality drive individual actions. *Bosses* actively seek the viewpoints of subordinates and attempt to learn what underlies the differing views. *Subordinates* who sense disagreement inquire about the boss's logic and open-mindedly follow up from there.

4

Transformation 2
Politics as Usual Won't Get You There

Chapter 3 presented the first of two transformations needed to make the switch from one-side-accountable, hierarchical relationships to two-sides-accountable relationships. Now we're going to discuss the second: changing how people think about political forces at work and how they conduct their politics. It's a topic we've been tracking for years.[1]

In this chapter we use three case examples to illustrate how switching from *false objectivity* and *politics as usual* sets the stage for emancipated, two-sides-accountable partnering, the relationship that breeds empowerment and trust. We expect you'll find the first two cases embodying lessons you can immediately apply. They reference situations you'll find familiar, if not for context then for their depictions of recognizable political dynamics. However we'll bet the ranch that you don't find much that's familiar in the final example. It's a big-time, business-to-business, two-sided accountability paradigm breaker. But first, let's take it from the top with the basics.

Politics is not a dirty word. It's what you get in any organization when people with different self-interests and different motivations, who actually see events according to those interests and

<hr />

[1]See Culbert and McDonough, *The Invisible War.*

motivations, hold a discussion for purposes of deciding what needs to be accomplished and who is going to do what. And, almost always, hierarchical structure is involved. In fact, effectively utilized, hierarchy constrains and channels political expression. It implies the format for reconciling the disagreements that naturally erupt as people "politically lobby" to get events named and priorities ordered in ways that facilitate their personal productivity and well-being.

But when people see the hierarchical structure failing to provide them the decision-making authority they require, to execute assigned responsibilities according to their distinctive competencies, they become reluctant to stand accountable. Fearing that they will become fall guys for decisions someone else made, they have little choice but to take their resistance underground, unleashing the manipulative, behind-the-scenes, buck-passing dynamics that give politics a bad name. What's a sensible person supposed to do when seeing him- or herself being set up to take the "hit" for a situation he or she felt forced to approach incorrectly? On the other hand, when the hierarchical structure embodied in the organization chart is articulated clearly, granting people sufficient authority to stand reputably accountable for the responsibilities assigned to them, politics function and reconcile with integrity.

Thus, organizational politics are neither good nor bad; they simply are. And, most importantly, you need to recognize that there's no avoiding them. People err when they ignore the existence of political forces and err when they eschew politics as categorically corrupt. But the biggest error comes in not realizing that politics are very personal and that their self-interested roots should be respected. People who fail to respect the personal, self-interested forces driving another individual's political behavior quickly see the need for the type of brute force constraints exemplified in one-sided accountability, boss-dominated relationships. This is what underscored the competitive, self-serving political dynamics manifest in each of the case examples presented in Chapters 1 and 2.

WHAT ARE "POLITICS AS USUAL"?

Examining hierarchical relationships for the political dynamics implied, we find bosses and subordinates caught up in a limited win-win paradigm that we label *politics as usual*. In this paradigm, the first win represents the pursuit of outcomes that are good for one's self; the second win represents the pursuit of outcomes that are good for the company.

Of the two, the first win, what's good for one's self, is far and away the strongest motive but, deceptively, is kept hidden. Instead, pursuing the second win, what's good for the company, is exclusively used in justifying all activities and efforts and in soliciting recognition for accomplishments. Ironically, the need to keep self-interests hidden produces a positive organizational dynamic as people are driven to find a work orientation in which self-interests and corporate pursuits overlap. Quickly people discover that framing self-interested pursuits as "doing what the company needs me to do" lessens the need for hierarchical domination and control. Instead of brute force directives—"Where are we going?," "How are we going to get there?," and "What are our priorities?"—discussions are held.

Organizational politics are created as people pursuing different *win-win* outcomes interact in their efforts to answer these questions in ways that fit their self-interests. To the extent that that two people see one another pursuing a reality that each perceives as self-beneficial, the politics are likely to be harmonious and compatible. But when people pursuing different win-win composites aren't immediately able to answer these questions in a reciprocally agreeable way, the political dynamics heat up and may become underground nasty. This is what takes place in hierarchical relationships when the boss, or more powerful party, is not knowledgeable or empathetic to the needs and concerns of an individual who feels one down.

Occasionally people orient to what's good for the company at the expense of what's good for themselves, perhaps out of disorientation, perhaps to buy credibility. However, self-sacrifice is an unstable situation and seldom lasts very long. Conversely, sometimes people orient to what's good for themselves but not good for the company. When they do so, they're smart to keep it under wraps since benefits stop and retributions begin once their self-focused indulgences are noticed.

Few set out to neglect other people's interests. It's just that looking out for other people can be an overwhelming and burdensome distraction for people trying to get somewhere else. It's hard enough to find a logic that aligns self-interests with those of the organization to a degree where others can't convincingly accuse you of putting your interests first. Making a spur-of-the-moment positive response to another person whose pursuits appear competitive is even more difficult.

In the heat of actual operations, finding out about other people and looking out for their interests becomes, at best, a secondary concern. Thus, the self-interested, politics-as-usual paradigm leads to a type of teamwork that, in practice, is more lip-service illusionary than real. It is political correctness over substance, with words to give the impression that everyone gains from what's being done despite the fact that personal compass settings are neither known nor publicly exposed.

Politics as usual, performed competently, are at best tactical, not strategic. All they buy is one situation at a time. They don't leave people who felt their interests were superceded by yours feeling good or trusting that, in a competitive moment, your motives will include looking out for their well-being, which is their central concern. They may not even leave people who benefited from your actions counting on benefiting the next time. They realize you don't know enough about their interests to make them a reliable part of your decision making.

Most people understand self-interested pursuits and try to take account of them in their organizational dealings. But what people don't stomach well is a lot of "doing it for the good of the company" and "personal sacrifice for team effectiveness" face work when noticing that their self-interests aren't in the mix. To be strategic, the politics you practice need to be relationship building. They need to engender trust. To accomplish this you need to add another "**win**" to the two "**win**s" driving your actions—a win for the other person. That is, being strategic requires that you operate in a **win-win-win** political paradigm.

YOU NEED TO PRACTICE A DIFFERENT TYPE OF POLITICS

Win-win-win is the transformation required for the two-sided accountability alternative to hierarchical relationships. This alternative is not for people who feel they must dominate to feel powerful or practice submission to feel safe. It's for people who want to hold direct and candid conversations—who are sufficiently secure to tell it straight and to encourage others to tell it back to them straight. It's an alternative that follows directly from a realization we had years ago[2] while observing successful managers. It's one we highlight in every leadership course we teach.

We tell students, "We know of no management tool that's more efficient than *a trusting relationship*. With trust, flawed systems and imperfect plans can be made to work; without trust the best system and the most perfectly conceived plan quickly become ineffective." Why? Because, as the bumper sticker reminds us, "stuff happens," and a trusting relationship is far more efficient than any command-and-control, carrot-and-stick tool for managing people who encounter ambiguity, adversity, misunderstanding, setback, surprise, and new opportunities when tackling a tough job, trying to do it "right." But how do people develop trusting relationships in a system laden with hierarchical expectations? With hierarchical relationships taken as the given, people miss seeing the core problem and thus miss seeing the obvious fix. Consider the following case.

---

[2]See Culbert and McDonough, *The Invisible War.*

SHORT CASE

The Salesman Who Comes in Late

Envision yourself the manager of men's furnishings in a major big-city department store. In the midst of a busy weekend-long sale, a normally dependable sales associate, without phoning, comes in two hours late. On arrival he immediately comes over to explain. Sounding defensive and inauthentic, he says, "At the last minute I realized I had a doctor's appointment, and by then I was too rushed to phone and say I'd be late."

How do you respond and why?

When we ask students, the majority give what we think is a too tough response, and most of the rest give one that, to us, seems too soft. The too tough responders pull rank. They use nicely worded innuendoes to put the salesperson on notice that a repeat could prove costly. The too soft go underground. They shrug off the salesperson's apology as if it were entirely unnecessary. However, upon questioning, they are quick to add their intention to document the incident meticulously for their "just in case it happens again" file, clearly indicating that their words of acceptance and belief are insincere.

From our perspective both responses are unnecessarily suspicious, patronizing, and hierarchical. Both miss the trust-building opportunities that the salesperson's *not* calling in provides. We advise students, "Put yourself in the salesperson's shoes. It makes almost no difference what the real situation was, whether there was a doctor's appointment, a fight with a girlfriend, or an errantly set alarm. The facts are that this normally dependable salesperson came in late without calling, which he knows is a violation, and you are face-to-face with an adult with whom you want to have a trusting relationship. Clearly, making a 'hierarchical' comment works against establishing a trusting relationship, and, as this story already demonstrates, making it will not stop what's unpreventable in the future."

Inviting self-reflection, we ask students, "If you were in the salesperson's shoes, what response could a department manager make to bridge the trust gap and the need for a fabricated excuse?" Identifying with the salesperson, their answers are often quite wonderful. They display a genuinely trusting character with comments that run something like, "I know you would have been here on time if that were possible—you're almost never late. If ever there's something I can do to help you out, please don't hesitate to ask." To our way of thinking a response like this would go a long way toward turning a hierarchical relationship into a relationship that has more trust and "in it together" accountability.

This case provides a vehicle for making four staccato points: trusting relationships are politically strategic; you can't achieve trusting relationships when operating with a hierarchical relationship mind-set; once you are immersed in a hierarchical mind-set, it's darned difficult to break out; and, even unilaterally invoked, a two-sided accountability mind-set can become a self-fulfilling prophecy.

There's an additional lesson in this case. In fact, we see it as the most essential one. **When you've got the capacity, stepping up and standing accountable for helping another person succeed is the politically smart thing to do.** It's smart for the organization, and it's smart in breeding reciprocal loyalty for yourself. What we're advising is more than a tactical show of empathy. We're advising that you maintain a constant lookout for opportunities, especially those available during setback and other moments of personal vulnerability, to help another person exercise his or her business responsibilities competently. This is what builds strategic, trusting relationships, the types that promote truth telling, goodwill reciprocity, and preventative problem solving. And we're not talking about forming a mutual protection society, which would be collusive against the organization. We're talking about recognizing that the organization reaps benefits from each individual who succeeds.

Our analysis of the situation faced by the department manager illustrates how hierarchical approaches ignite a cycle of suspicion such as the one that led the tardy salesman to propose a doctor's appointment as an excuse. The problem with one-side-accountable, hierarchical relationships is that both parties usually operate split-focused, with hierarchical concerns blocking the relationship-building opportunity at hand. The aforementioned case has a manager worrying about securing the command-and-control system and the subordinate worrying about his job, with hierarchical thinking subordinating human dimensions to organizational politics. Such a self-protective focus can only perpetuate a culture of distrust.

Illustrating how an individual's self-protective focus holds the potential to screw up a potentially rewarding relationship, we turn now to "The Case of the Negotiating Physician." We encountered this case while counseling a highly skilled and sought-after physician-researcher recruited to join the pediatric oncology team at a prestigious university hospital.

CASE 2

The Case of the Negotiating Physician

The physician told us that she liked everything about the position except that the money was a bit uncertain, and she wanted that uncertainty removed. The position had three components: administering to hospital patients, conducting and publishing research, and participating in a fee-for-service private practice. Although the salary was 30 percent more than her current pay, she didn't like that an additional component would come from joining her oncology colleagues in a private practice partnership with her income based on services she rendered. It didn't matter that this sum was over and above what already constituted a higher salary. For some idiosyncratic reason she objected to having this additional fee, which would take her pay way beyond her personal "happiness quotient," as a variable. She preferred the certainty and simplicity of a set, agreed-on, fixed amount.

Saying that she would tell the oncology group that she prided herself in pulling her part of any load and always going beyond duty's call, she asked us, "Do you see anything wrong in my asking them to make the entire package a fixed salary with nothing variable?" We saw everything wrong, especially her politics. We saw her demanding one-sided accountability from a partnership that hadn't given her "the power." We feared that her need for personal consideration, without consideration of the dilemmas her request might pose for the others, could provoke significant suspicion in a new relationship that needed trust.

We asked if she knew whether other physicians had such an arrangement. She responded, "No one does." She then changed the topic by adding that, when considered nationally, even the 30 percent higher fee was relatively low for someone with her research record and demonstrated ability. We asked, "Why do you suppose the fee for seeing private patients was set as a variable?" Rather naively, we thought, she answered, "I have no idea." Then we asked, "What do you suppose your prospective colleagues might fear that would lead them to resist a request to treat private patients for a fixed fee?" Again she couldn't conceive of their objections. Even with hypotheticals, she was so fixed on what she wanted that she couldn't try out their shoes.

We were surprised by how difficult it was for the physician to see the problem her prospective partners were trying to solve. Of course, we were trying to get her to see how they were guarding against any partner who might not pull his or her private patient weight. But she was too focused on her goal of getting a predictable income to marshal understanding for the mind-sets of the established physicians. While we found her myopia relatively extreme, we also were aware that, when viewed by uninvolved others, each of us possesses some obvious and blatant blind spots.[3]

One takes a perilous course when yielding to the temptation to give advice without actually knowing all the people involved. Nevertheless, we thought, a different type of offer might thread

---

[3]See Chapter 3 of Culbert, *Mind-Set Management.*

the needle between this physician's desires for a predictable figure and the concerns she was encountering. Hesitantly, we offered her the two-sided accountability script. We suggested that she voice her enthusiasm for joining the partnership and then explain some personal background factors that made her need for a predictable income understandable. We suggested that she then ask her prospective partners for an estimate of the monthly fees she might receive from work with private patients. We said, "If hypothetically it's $5,000, then offer them a three-month trial for $12,000, with the monthly fee to be renegotiated at that time. By that point your value and work ethic should be documented, and your sacrifice can be used to get you the somewhat larger predictable figure your competent work warrants." We counseled, "If you get a response that shows our assumptions to be invalid, then, as a backup strategy, you can ask your prospective partners to see if they can figure out a way to solve your dilemma, given your concerns." Of course, the bigger issue was circumventing her win-win, politics-as-usual focus to take a **win-win-win**-oriented action that the other physicians would see as credible. As it turned out, this physician got lucky. The partners accepted her offer and she signed on with high spirits feeling that she had professionally advanced into a high-status, good paying job.

THE POLITICS REQUIRED FOR TWO-SIDED ACCOUNTABILITY ARE WIN-WIN-WIN

Two-sided accountability is possible once two or more parties recognize that their individual interests overlap, believe that the other party's self-interested pursuits can be conducted in a way that furthers mutual objectives, and are able to articulate a way of working together that each believes to be reciprocally advantageous because the political process supports it. We've been talking **win-win-win** politics in which each party has committed him- or herself to support the other party's efforts and possesses enough knowledge about and appreciation of the personal roots driving that person's commitments to be supportive and behave respectfully. Thus, the third win represents more than the other party's organizational commitments; it embodies all the salient self-interested pursuits hidden in that person's composite win-win.

A relationship only takes on the character of two-sided accountability after the parties specify a collaborative plan with agreements about responsibilities and authorities including the responsibility to assist the other to succeed. Precisely which responsibilities are agreed to depend on the business activity. However, in most instances, two-sided accountability includes playing an active role in helping another party realize the self-interested gains that underlie that party's interest in the business endeavor. Sometimes one or both parties extend their concern to issues not covered by the business activity, such as making helpful suggestions regarding finances, the handling of an enfeebled parent, or other personal matters outside of work. When this takes place, a business relationship can lead to friendship and personal bonding, which in turn fortifies trust in the business relationship.

Two-sides-accountable relationships come with the general expectation that the parties will cooperate, act supportively, and be socially pleasant. Then, depending on the business activity, there are additional responsibilities. To the extent that each person sees the other exercising those responsibilities, the parties develop trust and confidence in one another. Of course, the amount of trust that's built depends on the complexity of the activity, the stakes attached to success and failure, and how the other person gets involved and pitches in during troublesome moments.

We think two-sided accountability obligates people to share all information pertinent to their business activity, to be honest and truthful in their dealings with one another, to perform functions as agreed, and to discuss business and perceived performance problems as soon as possible upon their being noticed. And because it takes considerable time and effort to terminate a relationship or to change reporting lines, the most efficient course is to commit to the other person's success. When someone fails to perform as you expect or as you believe the company needs for that person's responsibilities to be carried out, remember the lessons from Chapter 3! Refrain from discussing how you see the situation and what you think until after you've inquired about and gotten a good feel for how that person sees events and has the situation personally framed. Next, remember the underlying logic of **win-win-win** politics: the company wins only when all stakeholders succeed. A summary of the contrasting mind-sets is included in Table D.

Practicing **win-win-win** politics makes you accountable for overseeing your associate's activities, offering assistance as you think it needed, and actively engaging that person when you think essential assistance is being inappropriately refused. Our critique of the environmental cleanup company case, the first case described in Chapter 1, was based on this logic. We held the executives accountable for helping the nonperforming lab to identify and fix their problems, and we held the lab accountable for making their problems known. Two-sided accountability holds all parties in a partnership responsible for one another's successful performance and realization of self-interested stakes. It also holds each party accountable for making their problems and motivations known.

TABLE D CONTRASTING MIND-SETS: INTERNAL POLITICS	
One-Side-Accountable, Hierarchical Relationships	**Two-Sides-Accountable Relationships**
Politics as Usual	**Win-Win-Win Politics**
Bosses and subordinates alike pursue their interests with jurisdictionally constrained interpretations of what the company requires and needs from them. They justify their activities on grounds that they are performing properly and benefiting the company. Personal and self-beneficial twists to their efforts are subliminal and hidden. *Bosses* are suspicious of subordinates' self-interested agendas. *Subordinates* resent the indulgence of bosses who pursue transparently self-serving interests.	*Boss and subordinates alike* look for ways to conduct their self-interested, company-enhancing pursuits with consideration for like pursuits of those with whom they interact. *Bosses* respect the self-interested side of subordinates' work commitments, attempting to learn what they are and provide appropriate support. *Subordinates* are comfortable with their own and others' explicit self-interested pursuits if they align with company interests.

In seeing *two-sided accountability* as a mind-set that you can unilaterally implement to initiate high-quality, trusting relationships, we acknowledge that occasionally you will encounter people so competitively self-centered that they lack the capacity to give your interests sufficient focus. Inevitably time exposes their character. We believe the benefits of not dismissing a rejecting individual who may have the capacity to eventually respond positively to your stand-and-be-counted accountability overtures far outweigh the costs of occasionally being taken in. Sometimes people, such as the aforementioned negotiating physician, need you to go the extra mile in extending them your goodwill. Whether or not she would have received the benefit of the doubt from the physicians recruiting her without our counsel remains an unanswered question. Of course, we were afraid she might not.

While people and their self-interested pursuits are the direct beneficiaries of two-sides-accountable relationships, far and away the biggest beneficiaries are the companies whose interests they represent. Two-sided accountability provides corporate benefits of a scope that's unimaginable in one-side-accountable, hierarchical relationships. The following case portrays the activities of an executive whose commitment to standing accountable qualifies him as a business partnering genius. It graphically illustrates the gains a company can realize when people at the top commit to a business associate's success. Because of the public nature of the project involved, there's no need to conceal names. The account we present and the facts presented are limited to what we personally observed.

CASE 3

Big Time Business-to-Business, Two-Sided Accountability Case

Background

After two years of deliberating how to bid the payload for Teledesic's broadband worldwide satellite system, billed as the "Internet In The Sky," TRW acquiesced to the number Teledesic had been asking bidders to match. Carefully specifying contingencies, TRW agreed to Teledesic's $3 billion target. That number, when added to $6.5 billion for power and guidance systems, ground support, system integration and test, and launch vehicle, brought the entire project to $9.5 billion, the amount Teledesic executives believed investors would find attractive.

Space scientists at TRW's arch competitor, Hughes Space and Communications, had also spent two years stalking the project, in the end convincing themselves Teledesic's $3 billion goal was unrealistically low. Adopting a wait and see approach, their aim was to stay in the bidding game, hoping Teledesic would eventually get "realistic." But the TRW bid advanced the deal to the point where Teledesic was calling for a final number. With no time left, Hughes was hard-pressed to come up with a competitive figure.

The situation was one that Hughes had faced many times, but always within the boundaries of a normal, one satellite, $70 million to $100 million deal. It was commonplace for Hughes executives to find themselves in a price-competitive market, bidding whatever it took to get a contract, and figuring the actual cost after the deal was sealed. Practicing brinkmanship, they counted on technological and manufacturing cleverness to lower costs to levels where they could make a profit. In the few projects where they couldn't, they would rationalize their loss, claiming, "We did what we had to do to maintain our marketplace leader image."

Requiring up to 350 satellites, the Teledesic project involved dollars and unknowns of another scale. A miscalculation could bankrupt almost any company. On the other hand, being left on the sidelines presented a significant problem. Not being chosen would deprive Hughes of the financing required to tool up for the mass production needs of the twenty-first century and its industry-leading role. A new strategy and paradigm were needed.

Taking the Open Kimono Approach

Fortunately for Hughes, the executive in charge of bidding the Teledesic business had an eleventh hour inventive idea. Using aerospace industry jargon, he told his bosses, "We've got no choice but to take an 'open kimono' approach." Playing up his company's stature, he told Teledesic executives, "You are right in thinking that both TRW and Hughes are the industry leaders. But that's as far as the similarities go. While we excel in inventing breakthrough solutions and living up to our commitments, TRW excels in painting technological pictures using creative marketing presentations that excite the mind with promises they don't always deliver." Persuasively he argued, "We've done our homework, and we're convinced no one can give you the performance you desire using numbers like the ones that TRW bid. And we'd like the opportunity to let your technical people see this for themselves. All we need is a little time. Spend that time, and soon you'll be able to proceed with confidence knowing exactly what you need to do." Then the executive proposed the unthinkable. He offered to treat Teledesic as a full business partner and to begin by opening his company's books. He would show them costs and profitability calculations and share with them some of the proprietary and leading edge technical insights that Teledesic seemed to lack.

Teledesic executives were amazed by his open kimono offer and immediately called a bidding time-out. They reasoned, "What's a few weeks in a project that will take three years to complete when what Hughes proposes provides an immediate practical test of the economics we've been pursuing?" At $3 billion Teledesic was asking for satellites built at one-tenth the cost of any satellite that had ever been produced, each with ten times conventional capacity, with a production volume that in one year would eclipse what the entire industry had produced in the last twenty.

The first meeting with Teledesic's technical leaders succeeded in making skeptics into believers. Hughes's engineers displayed the system architecture that would allow Teledesic to achieve the performances they envisioned. Unbeknownst to Hughes, the TRW bid relied on a reduction in system capacity and lower quality customer service. The Hughes architecture caused Teledesic executives to believe that TRW had compromised too much in meeting their pricing bogey. They began to suspect TRW's technological know-how and judgment.

Cementing their attention, the Hughes executive set out to test TRW's pricing assumptions. Inviting Teledesic personnel to observe, Hughes engineers convened a "subcontractors' fair" in which a subsequently simplified, full-performance architecture was put on the table for potential subcontractor education and bid. Even with newly simplified requirements, a composite of the lowest, not necessarily the best, subcontractors' bids, including a nominal management fee and profit for Hughes, put the payload cost at more than $5 billion.

Then the Hughes executive divulged the rest of his plan. Hughes would continue to refine architecture and reconvene bidders every two weeks. He said the reconvening would feature an exchange in which subcontractors would be asked to explain what factors and contingency plans inflated their costs. The elicited comments would be used in reworking architecture with changes and revised architecture used as the basis for new bidding. The executive counted on this iterative process to get costs closer to Teledesic's target number.

While the name of the game was "iteration to drive costs down," the executive explained that Hughes also had a responsibility to protect its subcontractors. Extrapolating from the situation he just faced, the executive explained, "On a project like this, profits are not the sole motive. The prestige of being associated with this breakthrough project offers industry-leading stature that could lead some subs to understate costs. But we don't want subs with financial problems. A company that's forced to drop out will cause expensive delays, and a company that takes shortcuts to survive is a threat to the operating integrity of the composite system."

Teledesic executives found the Hughes initiative impressive both for its candor and quality of reasoning. By the end of the second subcontractor fair, they awarded Hughes the contract. Technologically they believed in Hughes's ability; sociologically they bought its two-sided accountability logic that your apparent success is fragile when the people you depend on are not succeeding.

Turning Competitors into Business Partners

The numbers were down to $3.8 billion, desirable subcontractors had been identified, and it was time to begin work. Since the architecture for the satellite system was not yet set, the contract would require flexibility. The words had to be firm enough to clarify what would be paid, sufficiently flexible to commit subs to lowering prices as architecture simplified, and conceptually clear enough to enable all parties to understand their agreements. Achieving the right mind-set was all the more important when considering that the unknowns and dollar amounts were, for most of the parties, enough to bankrupt their companies.

Recognizing the stakes and the flexibility required, the Hughes leader felt it essential to bolster subcontractor understanding and commitment. Issuing contracts he included a note stipulating that each contract was contingent on the subcontractor's presence at two days of executive-level briefings. Providing less than two weeks' notice, he requested that each subcontracting company send two representatives to an "Orientation and Business Partnering Meeting." For representatives, he asked for the top executive of the business unit working on this project, in most cases the company's CEO, and the executive in charge of production. The agenda was quite specific. After overviews by Teledesic and Hughes, it was almost entirely devoted to subcontractor presentations. Each subcontractor was allotted twenty minutes to address three issues. First, "Describe your company and what this project means to it." Second, "Describe the problems and technical challenges posed your company by this project." And third, "State actions that Teledesic and Hughes can take to aid your company's success."

Testifying to the importance of this project, attendance was perfect. Top-level executives arrived without any verbalized complaints about how this short notice meeting jarred their busy schedules.

As is the custom at Hughes, the executive previewed his presentation for his two bosses, the company president and the sector CEO. As described, these leaders had delegated the authority to him and had been diligent about involving him in all executive level discussions. They even shielded him from those in the company whose career ambitions lead them to interject themselves and act competitively.

Among the charts the executive wanted to present was one with revealing financial information that he felt was essential to establishing subcontractor trust. He said, "Only by taking the lead in walking the talk can we get our subs to really trust us." The CEO balked, saying, "No one expects to see our numbers, and showing them opens us to questions that I don't think we need to answer right now." Pushing back, the executive responded, "I know this isn't our usual way of doing things, but, given the trust level I want established, nothing less than full disclosure will do." Skeptically, the CEO went along.

Apparently both executives were correct. Subcontractor executives were speechlessly surprised when the Hughes numbers were shown. In the wrap-up, several explicitly said that they would never have been won over without Hughes showing them the figures that made them believe the partnering was nonexploitative and real. In particular, they were delighted to see that the pricing targets given them were consistent with the agreement Hughes had with Teledesic. They could detect no hidden reserve beyond the $250 million Hughes put on the table for helping subs in trouble. Subs claimed that if they had been told the number was this low without seeing the numbers given Teledesic, they would have left the meeting believing that Hughes was making out at their expense.

At the meeting, an early confrontation produced dramatic relationship bonding. It occurred immediately at the end of the Hughes overview, after the numbers had been shown. The executive displayed a chart listing the eleven discreet subsystems comprising a satellite's payload and the names of the two invitees that had been selected to produce that module, with a Hughes unit listed as backup. For example, two companies received contracts for building the same antenna, each given an allocation of 100 with a Hughes unit receiving an allocation for the residual 150. The executive stated that his goal was to minimize the Hughes production role. To achieve that, he needed one or both of the two subcontractors geared up to perform such high-quality work that Hughes could surrender its allocation. In the event of both doing a standout job, the extra allotment would be divided equally. Challenging the limitation of this logic, a subcontractor CEO asked, "How about my company doing such a good job of gearing up that you decide to award us the entire 350?" While appearing hostile to the other companies present, his question was based on sound logic. All executives in the room were, in other spheres, business competitors.

Going right to the question's core, the Hughes executive answered, "We're not going to ask anyone who is here today to leave the project. We feel that each of you has already invested a great deal and deserves to be in the deal." Starkly the implications sunk in. The game had changed! Suddenly each company had more to gain by thinking of their competitors as business partners. The path to technological security and bigger margins lay in eliminating duplication of subassembly steps and teaming up on problem solving and invention. Moreover, across the eleven constituent modules, twenty-two companies could divide up the workload, delegating problems that affected everyone to cross-company teams. For instance, working out the standard for hermetic seals would benefit nine of eleven subassembly modules.

The two days of presentations was complemented by informal interactions that had several CEOs requesting quarterly follow-ups. None had been anticipated, so a subcontractor executive nominated himself to take the lead in convening them. Quickly he established a list of common problems, such as coming up with a standard for hermetic seals, and called on each company to contribute an expert to join with Hughes engineers in creating it. Two weeks later subcontractor engineers were on-site at a Hughes location identifying and solving problems and making suggestions that further simplified the architecture. Meanwhile the phones and faxes were buzzing as subcontracting executives worked out profitable intramodule side deals.

TWO-SIDED ACCOUNTABILITY LESSONS

What the executive called the "open kimono" approach illustrates at least five demonstrations of two-sides-accountable partnering, with each instance reinforcing the impact and orientation achieved by the others. The first was the information-sharing activities that allowed Hughes to educate Teledesic on the actual costs of building the system and the process for getting those costs down. This action built confidence to the point that Teledesic executives awarded Hughes the contract without knowing what the exact cost would be. The second was at the "Orientation and Business Partnering" meeting when Hughes revealed its numbers. Showing the subcontractors the profitability they hoped to turn, including a $250 million reserve for possible subcontractor bailouts, made the nonexploitative dimension of the partnership real. The third instance took place when the Hughes executive publicly committed to each subcontractor's success by announcing that each would receive the same minimum allocation. The fourth instance took place when the Hughes executive indicated that he had intentionally left subcontractors an open door for profitability enhancements and risk management through side deals and technology sharing. And the fifth occurred when subcontractors were encouraged to participate in defining performance parameters and to suggest improvements in system architecture.

CONCLUSION

We have many stories bearing on the dynamics of **win-win-win** politics and two-sides-accountable relationships, and the organization benefits that result. Each month provides additional ones. On the other hand, we have a much bigger storehouse of cases illustrating money left on the table by people stuck in a hierarchical mode exerting one-sided accountability controls. In fact, that aforementioned open kimono approach eventually hit a troubled road when the CEO of Hughes, Mike Smith, and Teledesic's owner, the legendary Craig McCaw, got into a reciprocal one-sided accountability tug of war over a financing issue. From our observation post, the matter appeared more a result of hierarchical upbringing than substantive concern. This raises a pivotal question: How do people reverse years of socialization to acquire the skills, commitment, and discipline to adopt a two-sides-accountable mind-set? Furthermore, once they have the skills and commitment, how do they overcome semantic and personality incompatibilities, ego needs, and political competitiveness to carry partnering up activities to fruition? These are among the issues addressed in remaining chapters.

5

You Need a Two-Sided Accountability Mind-Set

By now we hope that you see hierarchical relationships as self-defeating prophecies and that your cultural predisposition for tolerating them has been significantly weakened. We also hope that *two-sided accountability* becomes your orientation of choice to the extent that daily you search for practical ways to implement it. Most people work under the illusion that hierarchical relationships ensure predictability and control. What's predictable is that hierarchical relationships are short-term, tactical approaches to getting work done and that the brand of control they produce leads directly to deception and self-justified dishonesty.

However, merely breaking your predisposition[1] for hierarchical relationships does not guarantee that you'll recognize a two-sided accountability opportunity when you see one or know precisely what to do when eyeing a situation where standing accountable for a boss's, a subordinate's, or a teammate's effectiveness would immediately lead to improvements in performance and dialogue. When people feel they must get things accomplished but don't know a way of proceeding that's different from the faulty way they have been using, they continue using the way they know.

---

[1]For a fuller explanation of what we think it takes for people to break their "set" predispositions for perceiving and valuing relationships, see Culbert, *Mind-Set Management.*

Until you internalize the prevalence and inevitability of subjectivity and the practicality of **win-win-win** politics, to begin thinking differently about what you do, you're going to find two-sided relationships unnatural. You may even feel ill at ease when others take the two-sided accountability initiative, changing how they relate to you.

Uncomfortable as it might be in the short term, we think you are better off feeling uncomfortable than denying what you know are the inevitable consequences of a hierarchical relationship. Believing that your job security and professional well-being depend on spinning and repackaging the truth for upper-level consumption, or thinking that lowers are deficient in comprehending the logic that's behind what you are out to accomplish, should now bother you to the extent that you actively seek an alternative. At the very least, we want you to see two-sided accountability as an alternative warranting serious consideration.

That's what this chapter is about. We want to reemphasize the benefits in candor and sensibility of action that are so readily apparent when people change from a hierarchical to two-sided accountability relationship and give you some practical application examples. Then we're going to consolidate the theory, hopefully adding to your confidence that you've got two-sided accountability sufficiently understood to be adventurous in utilizing it. Before we do this, however, we'd like to address a question that many people see as a major obstacle: What if the party you're trying to team up with fails to comprehend the advantages of two-sided accountability and what you're trying to accomplish? That is, doesn't it take two to make a relationship?

WHAT IF THE OTHER
PERSON DOESN'T GET IT?

Certainly your ability to form nonhierarchical relationships depends on what others are doing. After all, if a person is aggressively competing with you, is constantly domineering, or compulsively submits by never leveling with you, your capacity to restructure the relationship for two-sided accountability is severely limited. Isn't it?

Not necessarily. In fact, we see two-sided accountability as a thought process you can activate in any situation, regardless of how others are behaving. We think of it as a mind-set that leads to high impact actions, not a scripted interaction. As a mind-set, two-sided accountability becomes a self-fulfilling prophecy that heightens the chances that others will see you interested in their making out OK. Minimally, it reduces the possibility that they'll see you competing with them. Alternatively, you'll find some people who recognize what you are up to and want to reciprocate. At this point we call your attention to the play within the play—your own role in another person's attempts to reciprocate. Some people may have placed you in the category of "people not ready for two-sided accountability" and are dealing with you that way. Likewise, it's smart to give people you've concluded aren't ready for two-sided accountability another chance.

On the other hand, we've all learned there are limits to how effective we can be thinking and operating differently from the people around us. Using two-sided accountability, you should get further than you do right now. And, of course, when you're the boss, it's always good for the company when others see you trying. What's more, we believe you've got little to lose pursuing a two-sided accountability mind-set even with people who think and act hierarchically. To illustrate this point and the types of relationships you can build by unilaterally taking a two-sided accountability approach, consider three brief case stories. Each depicts how one person's change in mind-set led to positive outcomes otherwise not previously possible. To assist in your recognizing mind-set and attitudinal differences, we include Table E as a tracking reference.

CASE 1

The Degraded Upgrade

A friend whom we often use as a lunchtime sounding board approached us with what he referred to as a "victory story." He said, "Thanks to you guys, 'Charlie Chump' scored a big one." Then he related his story: "Last week I had to make an overnight trip to the East Coast, flying two days before

TABLE E CONTRASTING MIND-SETS: ACCOUNTABILITY	
One-Side-Accountable, Hierarchical Relationships	**Two-Sides-Accountable Relationships**
Bosses and subordinates alike act with a mind-set that the boss ultimately gets his or her way. *Bosses* evaluate subordinates without a system they see ensuring fairness or candid, reciprocal critique. *Subordinates* must answer effectiveness questions thought up and raised by the boss, with negative consequences for "wrong" answers. Feeling open-endedly vulnerable, they seek "to purchase" a generous interpretation through deferential behavior.	*Bosses and subordinates alike* recognize the bosses' authority to make decisions, but still act on a mind-set that each person on the "team" is answerable to the others. *Bosses* act accountably to all "teammates" who have a stake in the decisions they make, or results that they are charged with producing, regardless of hierarchical level. *Subordinates* take the initiative in requesting information and perspective on all topics that concern them. They think the boss's job includes staging for their personal effectiveness and success as well as concern for their development.

Thanksgiving. Anticipating an overcrowded plane, I decided to call United's Premier hot line to request an upgrade to business class. They confirmed the request and assigned me seat 5A.

"Arriving at the airport, I was confronted with a jungle. The terminal was undergoing construction and jammed with holiday travelers. Weaving my way to the gate, I discovered that there had been an equipment problem, and my flight was delayed an hour. Waiting in the long line, I rationalized that at least I'd be able to stretch out comfortably on the plane.

"When I finally reached the desk, I gave my name and presented my coupons for upgrade. The United person looked at the computer and said, 'All that's left are middle seats in the back.' Protesting that I was in business class and already had a seat assignment, she said, 'Your name is not on the list, all the seats are already assigned, and there is absolutely nothing I can do.' I explained that I had been confirmed by 'Premier reservations.' She then asked, 'What's the name of the person who confirmed your upgrade?' When I responded that I didn't remember, she

gave me a look that made it appear as if she had totally im-
peached my story.

"I thought, 'What difference does it make that I don't know the
person's name? You just told me there were no more seats. What
difference could it make whether I remembered the reservation
person's name? Were they going to call her to find out whether
she remembered me and that it was she who made the error?
Would they call someone to whom they had already given an
upgrade back to the podium to take back that person's seat and
give it to me? No way!'

"I was just going to do my loudmouthed, Neanderthal-ugly 'I
want to see your supervisor' thing when I remembered your admonition 'Don't take all the responsibility for solving problems
you lack the resources to fix. Make the other person your partner; let them help you solve it.' By this time I was pretty worked
up and felt that I might have alienated the person looking up my
reservation, so I turned to her associate who had been listening
in on our discussion. Forcing myself to be polite, I asked, 'What
would you do in my situation—how would you solve my problem?' In response, she punched something into her computer,
took my ticket and coupons, and punched some more letters.
Then she handed me a boarding pass for a different gate and
said, 'You'd better move quickly; I just booked a business class
seat for you on a flight that leaves in ten minutes. This flight
probably won't leave for another two hours.'

"Well, do you guys believe this one? There's not one doubt in
my mind that if I hadn't turned to her for help, she wouldn't
have said a thing, and I'd have been 'sardined.'"

While this is not an "organizational" story per se, the interaction dynamics are the same. Feeling beaten by the preliminary outcome, our friend's first impulse was to assume a hierarchical
relationship. Intimidation was his inclination, a first-rate, rank-
pulling, hierarchical relationship response. He was primed to go
Neanderthal combative despite a lifetime of experiences telling
him this is not the best way to motivate an individual to help you

out, especially a person whose behavior you can't control. And the outcome probably would be self-defeating. Watching a colleague attacked is not the best way to inspire someone to help.

The next case illustrates the personal connection that is needed for an individual to assume a two-sided accountability mind-set and to make it so prominent that other types of relationships no longer make much sense. It shows how, once **win-win-win** politics are initiated, reciprocity is forthcoming from people who don't necessarily comprehend the motivations behind your action.

CASE 2

Cooling Mr. Ferocious's Jets

Actually it's a bit of a misnomer to call the subject of our case "Mr. Ferocious," because the executive we're about to describe was also quite kind and oftentimes quite approachable. But his boss had been bombarded with complaints, and that's what caused her to reach out to us for help. She told us, "When dealing with subordinates, he's nothing less than ferocious. When he sees someone performing incompetently, he'll get right in the guy's face and shout. He gets along well with those above him, but even with us he can lose his composure. The first time he lost it with me, I looked him right in the eye and said, 'Do you really want me to cry?' Now when he comes on aggressively I laugh him out of it. Sometimes I cross my eyes, which always breaks him up. Sometimes I throw my arms up in the air in an act of mock surrender. Other times I grab a tissue and pretend to loudly blow my nose. Then, in an instant we're back to sober give-and-take. We tried promoting him to a position where he couldn't upset so many people, and we even gave him a company car. But the customer he serviced loves him and threatened to withdraw his account if he couldn't work with him. Since that customer is responsible for 20 percent of our business, we returned him to his former position, but now he won't return the car."

Knowing Mr. Ferocious had a reputation for getting right to the point, we wryly began our first meeting by saying, "We're the guys your boss sent to fix you." But before we could tell him that we weren't going to function as his boss's operative, Mr. Ferocious said, "I welcome the help."

To our inquiry "Why?" he responded, "You guys have people's respect. I have a lot to gain by having you on my side. I need someone with an independent voice to vouch for how screwed up our operations have become. As you know, my job as national accounts manager is to provide bridges between customers and the company. On one side, I help the customer formulate and advance his marketing agenda; on the other, I help our creative and production groups first to understand what the customer wants and then to get it produced. But there are just too many times when our people disregard what I tell them or lose track of the customer's priorities and schedule. It's as if our company goes out of its way to hire incompetents."

Referring to his boss, we said, "Joan says sometimes you lose it. What's that about?" The question ignited his ire, and he proceeded to demonstrate the point. He went into a fifteen-minute tirade describing thoughtless actions and work unit mistakes. Listening to his examples, however one-sided they might have been, left us with the impression that his company's operations could use some fixing.

We told Mr. Ferocious, "We can't fix operations, but we do have some ideas about how you could get your messages across more effectively." We asked rhetorically, "Do you typically get the response you are looking for from a person you've just let have it?" Before he could answer, we loaded on a second question: "How do you think a subordinate receiving one of your admonishments winds up feeling about you?" Mr. Ferocious didn't answer, which told us that for a moment we had him reflecting on what was self-defeating. To his credit he resisted coming out with the old "they have it coming to them" response. Nevertheless, it was clear that Mr. Ferocious needed a new script. Seeing pictures of two children on his desk, one apparently with a disability, provided an idea.

We said, "Scotty, let's say one of your boys was clearly capable of getting all A's and the other had a learning disability that made getting C's quite difficult. Wouldn't you treat them differently?" Mr. Ferocious opened up. He replied, "Sure, I'd hound the first and praise the second." Asking him what he meant by "hound," he described a badgering process that resembled what his boss described as his behavior with the people he called "incompetent." We then asked him how he would treat a son who had a disability. His answer was terse and, we thought, quite wonderful. He said, "Well, that's the type of kid who needs points just for trying because you know he's going to be subjected to a lifetime of setbacks and failures. That kid needs his self-esteem supported. I would try to give him lots of encouragement. I'd try to praise whatever he did, particularly when he worked hard and failed to get a good grade."

Quickly summarizing, we said, "You mean it's OK to withhold praise when an achieving son brings home a B while the rest of his grades are A's, and it's OK to praise the other son for sticking at it in courses where his grades are less than C?" He said, "When you put it that way, I guess that's what I said, but I also know that everybody needs support and appreciation." To emphasize his point, we asked, "Everybody?" He answered, "Yeah, everybody, even me. Single-handedly I'm holding together a $100 million account, and all I ever hear from my management is how the incompetents complain about me, and I'm not entitled to the car."

Then we said, "Here's an idea. Think of everybody whom you see screwing up as a person with limitations struggling to perform competently. Give those people all the support and encouragement you can. And when they fail to act or think as you expect, remember to assume they are doing their best and that your job is to discover the reasoning that led them to an action that would never have occurred to you. Resist your inclination to assume that their reason is a lame excuse for overlooking your customer's priority; frame your inquiry to find out what greater priority led that person to take a different course. See if you can discover what personal resource or limitation made it difficult for him or her to respond the way you thought best. And each time you find yourself about to unleash on someone, try to think about this person as you would a child who needs support and guidance to be his best."

Scott's boss had been using a hierarchical "I insist that you change your behavior" approach in trying to persuade him to stop overpowering people. If she had succeeded, we never would have been asked to help. Her hierarchical approach didn't work. You don't change someone's hierarchical actions by acting hierarchically. We gave Scott a practical win-win-win metaphor that seemed to touch him emotionally, an essential condition for someone changing his behavior. It provided a bridge to "the nice guy" part of Scott, a part he wasn't always able to access. Apparently Scott had gotten up the organizational ladder as a self-interested power taker. We were looking for a compelling logic that would cause him to power share. Now, a year or more later, whenever we bump into Scott he finds some clever way of telling us, he still uses the child-in-need metaphor. And whenever we see his boss, she reminds us of how our work with Scott taught her to form more personally collaborative relationships with subordinates who need to grow before they can change.

CASE 2

Holding Off the "Attorney from Hell"

Walking through the executive suite, we dropped by the office of an executive who kept stock quotations on his computer monitor, some of which were interesting to us. Peeking in the door we could see him on the phone, fuming. He waived us in. We amused ourselves by looking at his screen. All the numbers were green, so we concluded that this wasn't what was upsetting him. As he hung up the phone, we attempted to lighten the atmosphere, quipping, "We dropped in for a drive-by shooting, but it appears somebody beat us to it." He responded, "I'm OK. It's just that this damn corporate attorney is getting to me. We're working hard to firm up a joint venture, and she seems to be working equally hard to screw it up. I'm about to ask my boss to get her reassigned."

He went on to explain: "I'm trying to build a trusting relationship while she's trying to 'bulletproof' the deal. Her one-sidedness is profoundly embarrassing. It's to the point that in order to pro-mote harmony with our joint venture partners, we have to join them in joking about what she's going to do next to destroy our deal. Behind her back we refer to her as 'our attorney from hell.'"

Responding, we argued, "Of course, you realize you're far better off getting her to join the team than knocking her off of it. Getting adversarial quickly becomes an exercise in pitting your friends against hers. That's going to consume a lot of your time. Anyway, it's partially your problem that you can't figure out a way to get her to join your team. He nodded, "I know you're right. I'll see what I can do." We then suggested, "How about giving her the problem? Ask her to fix the deal. Then she'll have to find out what you guys want."

Two weeks later the executive called to tell us about a "love-in" he held with his joint venture partner, the partner's attorney, and his attorney, who, he said, was "no longer from hell." At that meeting he and his partner presented their individual business objectives with the joint request that the two attorneys put their heads together to figure out a deal that would work. He told us, "Now the two attorneys walk around holding hands, acting as if they are solely responsible for turning an impossible business situation into a great deal for both companies. In the process I learned a lot about what was wrong with the deal my partner and I were trying to close. There were several important issues that I hadn't fully appreciated."

This story illustrates how operating with a two-sided accounta-bility mind-set can create alternatives to hierarchical relationships even when it seems like no alternative exists, when it seems like one of the parties is locked into a hierarchical mind-set. It shows how readily two-sided accountability sometimes can be accom-plished if someone knows how to make the first move, in this case by nonjudgmentally and noncombatively inviting the other party to lead the problem solving teamwork.

Implied is another point that's not as apparent as the first. People immersed in hierarchical relationships and hierarchical thinking are inclined to make responses that cause others to relate hierarchically. In this instance our executive buddy had assumed that the attorney was incorrigible and wanted to go the command-and-control hierarchical route in ridding himself of her resistance. All we contributed were some stand-accountable cues and the logic that "taking her out" would be time-consuming and emotionally draining. Apparently, little else was needed.

Taking these cases as a set, we'd like to emphasize a couple of very important issues.

First, *two-sided accountability* **is more a** *mind-set* **that generates behavior than a behavioral algorithm you discipline yourself to use.** This means your attitude about people and how you actually think about the business relationships you form is far more important than any particular sequence of actions you might program yourself to take. In fact, a scripted sequence of actions is likely to come across as inauthentic and generate suspicion that you're acting hierarchically.

Second, **you can invoke the** *two-sided accountability mind-set* **unilaterally**. Each of these cases portrays two-sided accountability as a mind-set phenomenon describing how people can self-invent actions that turn relationships around. They demonstrate how people can break from the impulse to transact hierarchically. Our friend gave the United Airlines person the opportunity to solve his problem. Mr. Ferocious found logic to override his impulse to use intimidation to get what he wanted. And the executive developed the perspective he needed to provide his "attorney from hell" a more appealing address.

PUTTING IT TOGETHER: ACHIEVING TWO-SIDED ACCOUNTABILITY

Now it's time to pull it together. We want to explain how the transformations presented in Chapters 3 and 4 connect and how instrumentally they produce the two-sided accountability mind-set. This mind-set leads to practical actions one could take in virtually any situation, even when interacting with people that have a hierarchical relationship proclivity.

How does one acquire a two-sided accountability mind-set? What thinking about people, teamwork, and organization gets you there? We have this broken down into three major principles, presented here with clarifying tenets. Taken together, these principles and tenets provide the foundation for acting more realistically and less duplicitously with the people you need to team up with at work. They set you on the bedrock foundation needed for avoiding and improving upon hierarchical relationships.

PRINCIPLE 1: INEVITABLE SUBJECTIVITY

In Chapter 3 we introduced the principle "organization is an artifact of the mind that views it," the subject of a previous book.[2] Succinctly stated, it holds that everything pertaining to an individual's activities at work is a matter of individual perception, inextricably influenced by the needs, interests, motives, means, and agendas of the individual viewing it. It's our way of saying, "What you see depends on where you stand." It's the story of the six blind men feeling different parts of an elephant being asked, "What is the object you are touching?" It's the story of the three baseball umpires bragging about the magnitude of their power when determining balls and strikes, with each umpire competing to outdo the others. The first umpire claims, "I call 'em the way I see 'em"; the second, "I call 'em the way they are"; and the third providing the topper: "They ain't nothing till I call 'em." In other words, subjectivity colors every aspect of an individual's life at work. Recognizing this allows you finally to resolve the question of what constitutes "reality" in a human endeavor. It alleges that each individual sees and interprets events distinctively and differently according to his or her motives, needs, and means.

Inevitable subjectivity posits that people are biased perceivers even when giving what they believe are honest accounts about what

---

[2] See Culbert, *Mind-Set Management.*

they experience and see. Internalize it and you'll stop fighting human nature. You'll no longer be put off by people who view and think about events differently than you do. And you'll have a way of figuring out where people are coming from when you try to influence them, especially when what you want them to do is not something they naturally think of doing. By considering that each individual lives within a unique reality, inevitable subjectivity is the ultimate diversity approach. It considers all individuals to be unique and distinctive; it treats all categories and stereotypes with suspicion.

This principle has the potential to turn your way of viewing people and organizational events inside out. Seeing things differently, you'll act differently. You'll understand the importance of accessing the deeply psychological and personal issues that underlie an individual's perspectives on events and relationships at work. You'll change the way you approach people you want to influence. You'll choose the right people as partners. You'll approach those you choose intelligently and sensitively.

The First Tenet of Inevitable Subjectivity

You can't tell exactly what an individual is doing or thinking merely by observing that person and his or her actions. We can go even further. When you are critical of someone's behavior, there's little likelihood that he or she is up to the same thing you would be up to if exhibiting the same behavior.

To understand exactly what someone is doing, you need to ask that person, "What are you up to, and why are you going about it this way?" If what you learn doesn't make sense, it means that you need to inquire further. For all questions we recommend you proceed with the tone of asking a "reasonable person." Instead of asking, "Why are you doing that?" or "Don't you know a more effective way?" as if the person is a dope, you need to think—and to express—"I'd really like to understand what you had in mind when you did what I would never think to do."

With a mind-set that assumes the person to be reasonable, your goal is to uncover the reasoning behind his or her actions.

For example, if the person seems unnecessarily suspicious about a deal he or she is making, you might say something like, "In your shoes I would be less suspicious, maybe even naive. What alerted you that got your guard up? I must have missed seeing it." If you still don't uncover the sensitivity, it's time to ask for more background. You might continue, "Is your reaction a typical one for you? What's taking place here that evokes it?" If, after asking such questions, you still don't understand why this person is "reasonably" reacting with suspicion, it's time to consult a mutual friend. But the bottom line is that it's not you filling in the blanks. If you do, you will only be stating why, under similar circumstances, you would do what the other person did, which you already know you would not. If you were similarly inclined, this issue would have never become a topic for your inquiry. There would be nothing more you needed to understand.

The Second Tenet of Inevitable Subjectivity

When you're not able to ask people what spurred them to act as you just observed, *your best way of understanding their intentions is to assume that they are doing what they feel they must in order to perform competently, the way they know how to be competent.* However, beware of tunnel vision. Assuming that people are primarily out to perform competently *at work* is shortsighted. To maintain political face, people talk as if everything they are doing is aimed at producing a competent work performance, but what's actually driving them is the idea of performing competently in their life more generally. People are interested in optimizing total life performance, and work events represent only one dimension, however important that dimension may be.

Your reluctance to assume that people whom you judge to be flawed in their dealings with the task at hand are doing their best to perform competently and to recognize that their focus includes many more issues than the work topic on which you are focused will cause you to systematically undervalue what people are doing. Thus, when spotting someone whose actions are, in your estimation, insufficient to the work agenda at hand, you should know it's time to start learning. Reflect on everything you know about that person's life and the strengths he or she is endeavoring to display, the flaws the person doesn't want exposed, and his or her personal expressiveness needs. Learn whatever you need to learn to make your understanding of his or her actions compute. Think about how a person with that individual's personal agenda and operating style could reasonably go about accomplishing what you see needing to be done. Whatever you do, don't start thinking that you know enough to get heavy-handed. There will be times you feel the urge, but it's an urge that needs resisting. Heavy-handedness is a one-way street toward cementing an adversarial hierarchical relationship in which stand-and-be-counted accountability takes a back seat to domination and control.

The Third Tenet of Inevitable Subjectivity

Everyone, including yourself, gives self-interested interpretations to all events, particularly ones that hold important personal consequences. Consistently we find this to be a principle that many people can't seem to behaviorally comprehend. Incorrectly, people make evaluative statements about the pluses and minuses of another individual's performance as if their assessment were perfectly objective. But careful scrutiny will show you that their assessment is greatly colored by what they have at stake personally. People cavalierly portray another person's predilections and biases as flaws that need correcting, not acknowledging that everyone they know views the world with biases and omnipresent self-interests and that the reason they are complaining about this individual's behavior is linked to their own self-interested motives. With this principle internalized, no critique of anyone else is complete without the phrase "and this gets in the way of my self-pursuits and interests." Not accepting this principle implies that somewhere there's a cadre of people whose work behavior is even handed and objective. Of course, the inevitable subjectivity principle critiques such presumption as spurious reasoning.

You'll find that your IQ for engaging in two-way accountability increases considerably when you internalize the fact that you, just like everyone else, are a self-interested and biased judge of other people's behavior. Given fair-minded values, you'll take this into account when considering your judgments. Instead of contending that the other person is doing something profoundly insufficient, you'll give more consideration to how actions taken by that person make matters more difficult for you. Of course, given your political sensitivity, you'll prudently choose the moments for publicly owning up. There are many times that you'll correctly choose to keep your self-effacing comments to yourself. There will be other times when you'll see that owning up allows others to experience you as someone they're willing to trust.

PRINCIPLE 2: PRACTICE
WIN-WIN-WIN POLITICS

If organizational behavior was a logical science, then all laws would follow from the law of self-interest: people interpret their jobs and perform their work in ways they perceive best for them. This premise features self-interests as a given with people seeking win-win outcomes. The first win features outcomes that benefit the individual, the second, outcomes that benefit the organization and the company. If, hypothetically, there were 6,431 outcomes that could benefit an organization, then each individual pursues a subset of 1,260 that also benefit him- or herself. This is why, when asked to explain their actions, people almost always have an explanation that emphasizes benefits to the organization.

But because different people possess quite different needs, desires, and capabilities, their self-interested pursuits are different. This quickly gets us to the first implication of the law of self-interests: **People with comparable assignments see their jobs differently and, because of this, pursue different avenues of action and reasoning when performing their work.** In our hypothetical, this means that two people working on parallel assignments will pursue somewhat different "1,260s." Moreover, in most instances, you can predict that they will interpret the other person's lack of overlap as neglecting an essential organizational interest. A second implication holds that **organizational dynamics leading to conflict derive from different people pursuing different interests in different ways.** Others hold that **the organization prospers when each member's self-interested pursuits are nested to augment the self-interested pursuits of other members** and that **enterprise activities are most efficient when staged to accrue rewards to all who participate.** Conversely, **people and their organizational endeavors stall and suffer when one of more of the constituents' interests are not addressed or adequately served.** Of course we're talking percentages since, from time to time, there are many organizational endeavors in which interests left out of the immediate mix receive focus in another endeavor or at a later time.

Simply stated, **an organization succeeds when people engaged in self-interested pursuits choose and perform activities in ways that are attentive to the needs of work associates and the organization.** In essence, we're saying that wherever possible, all organization actions ought to be predicated on **win-win-win** reasoning, with the first win being the interests of the individual taking action; the second, the interests of corporate entity, and the third, the interests of others affected by that action. Of course, practically speaking, we know that people won't always be able to figure out how to act in ways that meet three sets of interests simultaneously. Nevertheless, we are talking about all three receiving active, intelligent consideration, especially when the end-game goal is two-sides-accountable, trusting relationships.

PRINCIPLE 3: PUT TWO-SIDED ACCOUNTABILITY INTO ACTION

Problems related to one-sided accountability were raised in Chapter 2, and we revisit them here from the vantage points of the antidote and treatment. Chapter 2 portrayed one-sided accountability as intrinsically hierarchical, with the implication that inevitably it leads to corruption and self-inflation.

Subsequently, we added the obvious, that one-sided accountability is anathema to open, honest, aboveboard, trusting relationships. One-sided accountability allows uppers to hold lowers' feet to the fire without lowers being able to complain that their feet are too hot. Of course, the reason behind our tirade is that we favor two-sided accountability. That is, we think every boss's job includes staging for the effective performance of the people he or she oversees. Who is better positioned than the performer to comment on the help and support that's needed and received? We crave partnerships instead of hierarchical relationships, and we eschew situations in which a boss gets to say how a subordinate is doing without the subordinate having a voice that counts.

We believe a company prospers most when bosses make it possible for everyone to work at his or her best. And we believe the method for affecting this is the establishment of reciprocal accountabilities. This implies inevitable subjectivity consciousness and **win-win-win** politics practiced at every level. Subordinates need to stand accountable for alerting all levels of "bosses" to structural constraints they think limit their ability to say candidly what they sincerely believe. Supervisors need to stand accountable for their efforts to oversee quality fairly and open-mindedly and provide coaching that's appropriately formatted for specific individuals. Managers need to stand accountable for their efforts to check and revise systems that are supposed to facilitate the effectiveness of units and groups. And leaders need to stand accountable for the effectiveness of organizational initiatives that leverage the resources of the people performing work and to facilitate their doing what they think the company actually needs done. All this requires reciprocity of effort and each individual focusing on how his or her way of tackling an assignment impacts every other person on the "team"—**win-win-win** politics.

SUMMARY

As a package, the three principles, with tenets and implications (summarized in Table F), lead to an accountability mentality that casts hierarchical relationships as an invalid default setting. One or

TABLE F	TWO-SIDED ACCOUNTABILITY PRINCIPLES
Principle 1	**There's no getting around it; subjectivity is inevitable.** Everyone interprets events distinctively according to his or her motives, needs, and means.
Tenet 1	**Don't guess what others are doing—ask them.** You can't tell for sure what someone is trying to accomplish, or why he or she is proceeding in a certain way, merely from observing that person's actions. This is particularly important to remember when you see someone doing what you would never prescribe. The best way to find out what that person is doing and why is to ask how he or she sees the situation and what they believe their actions will accomplish? Only after you hear the explanation and seek to understand it in the context of the person's intentions and motivations can you voice your opinion in a way that's likely to be accurately heard and possibly well received.
Tenet 2	**Until you can ask, assume others are trying to be "life"-competent.** When you aren't able to inquire directly, assume the individual is doing what he or she feels must be done in order to perform "life" competently, the best way that person knows how to do it. Interpret the other person's motives broadly, not restricted to the task at hand.
Tenet 3	**Remember that "everyone" includes yourself.** You also view organizational events self-interestedly, constantly scrutinizing for "life" benefits, opportunities, and threats.
Principle 2	**Practice win-win-win politics.** At work, any statement or action, taken or perceived, that affects someone's ability to function effectively is "political." Conducting one's politics strategically entails active consideration of what each interacting party has at stake. We call the orientation of searching for self-interested outcomes that also benefit others the win-win-win orientation to organizational politics. The first two wins include what's self-beneficial and what benefits the company; the third win is what others deem important to their interests and success. Leaving out any of the three reduces one's political motives to tactical, resulting in a pull back toward hierarchical relationships.
Principle 3	**Put two-sided accountability into action.** Look for opportunities to initiate, build, and sustain two-sided accountability relationships, particularly in interactions you have with a boss or subordinate.

more of these principles were critical elements in each of the cases related and the success people had in converting contentious relationships to ones breeding trust and confidence. This chapter was on individual effectiveness, and you certainly should have seen the applications of these principles in them. The next chapter is on the topic of group effectiveness and teamwork, dynamics greatly valued today. There you will see how acceptance of subjectivity and **win-win-win** politics leads to a rethinking of what constitutes true teamwork and the mind-set required for this type of teamwork to be achieved.

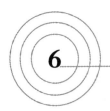

6

Team Effectiveness Requires It

We hate to say this and wish it weren't true, but most of the teamwork we've seen in our consulting is the naive "snap-to-gether" kind. Pun intended, it's the "staff infection" that results from people reasoning with false objectivity and practicing self-interested politics. It's how people entrenched in a hierarchical relationship system customarily operate. Snap-together is also the type of teamwork we find students using in the MBA courses we teach, always with mixed results.

You know how snap-together teamwork goes. Upon receipt of a group assignment, a project team meets to divide the work and agree on the approach they'll use. Usually it's an amicable, time-efficient meeting in which each individual takes pains not to be seen playing a strong-willed role in pushing a direction, role, or any concern that might reveal a personal motive. Most often work gets distributed by load, sometimes by expertise, and inevitably, there's subliminal maneuvering as people endeavor to get time frames and assignments aligned with personal scheduling needs, always without saying much about those needs. Then, shortly before the assignment is due, with time running out, there's a meeting aimed at *snapping together* the individual contributions into a coherent whole. But inevitably the group members' individual accomplishments don't quite match up and mesh.

While each scenario is different, there's a pattern to how efforts that don't match up are handled. Typically someone who is seen as having made a stellar effort confronts an outlier saying something like, "I thought you understood what we needed and what you were supposed to do. What you've produced isn't sufficient and doesn't fit in." On the defensive, the outlier responds, "I did precisely what I said I was going to do. You heard my words— why didn't you say something then?" By this point emotions are heating up, and others chime in registering their agreement with the mainstream confronter. Then, often more as an expression of personal loyalty than actual agreement, someone will say, "You guys are being much too hard on Jason. I can see how he might have gotten the impression that we wanted what he produced." It's at this point that a heroic individual, usually someone who disdains conflict, says, "This haggling isn't getting us anywhere. I can rework what Jason produced to make it fit." Because time is at a premium, and people are relieved that the problem at hand has been stopgap-solved, the group goes along with the hero's proposal. But everyone also knows the final product will be patchwork and that the group's potential will not be realized.

It's often the same in industry. Team members with multiple project involvements, reasoning with false objectivity and practicing self-interested politics, strive to work efficiently. Inevitably, they wind up missing one another, quibbling about who is wrong, and at the end, rushing to cobble together pieces that don't mesh smoothly. To deal with tensions in the aftermath, palliatives are administered in the form of team-building retreats, 360-degree feedback, and other rapport-building activities intended to help people feel better about one another's motives and reestablish fluid dialogue. But back in the daily swing of things, the forces unleashed by hierarchical relationships again erode esprit de corps.

SNAP-TOGETHER TEAMWORK RESULTS FROM ONE-SIDED ACCOUNTABILITY

Snap-together teamwork holds the potential to produce team efforts that subtract from what each person accomplishes individually. It involves the same one-sided accountability dynamics one finds in boss/subordinate hierarchical relationships: one party attempting to hold another accountable for an unsolved problem without recipro-cally standing accountable for not creating the circumstance in which the allegedly guilty party could perform more effectively. This was the underlying dynamic in the three problematic situa-tions described in Chapter 5. Each readily corrected once the indi-vidual who felt outraged by the other party's failed performance was prompted to use a two-sided accountability mind-set. Had our friend who believed the United Airlines agent had abrogated the airlines' accountability to him gone Neanderthal-ugly, acting as if he had no responsibility to comport himself respectfully, he would have had a "sardine-ized" flying experience. Had Mr. Ferocious continued to hold project people accountable for not giving suffi-cient focus to what customers wanted, without standing account-able for eliciting their cooperation, he would have continued being stereotyped "skull and cross-bones toxic." And had the executive who was about to use hierarchical, command-and-control tactics on the lawyer he perceived fighting him not stood accountable for po-sitioning her to be a value-added player, he would have wasted en-ergy needlessly on a crusade to vanquish her.

From our viewpoint, it's not the outlier's laziness or disorien-tation that causes the problem. Whether we're talking about an MBA project or a project group at an advertising agency, the real culprit is the naiveté of people who automatically think that oth-ers will perform as they expect. Once again we're back to critical, but seldom internalized, lessons about the inevitability of subjec-tivity and diversity and about internalized understanding that the same words uttered and listened to by different people seldom communicate a common meaning. These are the very issues that lead executives and students alike to answer incorrectly our "using what you know about human nature" questions described in Chapter 3. The students in our "hypothetical" should have known they weren't going to wind up on the same page and never should have bought the pretense that their words would communicate universal meaning. With *inevitable subjectivity* awareness they would have remembered that people, especially those with whom they hadn't worked before, always think and operate differently than they expect. Practicing ***win-win-win politics***, and seeking ***two-sided accountability*** relationships, they would have recognized that oversight and collaboration are best performed as front-end activities engaged in prior to a project's beginning.[1]

With future managers experiencing snap-together teamwork training like this, it's no surprise that we usually see the same kind of teamwork arrangements in industry. On the other hand, occasionally someone's unschooled and natural inclinations cause that person to do it better. For example, take young Magic Johnson.

Magic Johnson Knew

In the fall of 1981, eleven games into his third season with the Los Angeles Lakers, twenty-three-year-old Magic Johnson made sports headlines by convincing the team's owner to fire the coach. Actually the Lakers weren't doing that badly; in fact, they had won seven games. But Magic's gripe went deeper than four losses. He was incensed that the coach insisted on a deliberate, half-court playing style that Magic saw ill suited to individual and team strengths. He believed his and his teammates' distinctive abilities were best used in a spontaneous, fast-paced offense that he should direct. Having spent half the previous season sidelined with an injury and watching from the bench, Magic was confident that he knew the other players' strengths. He wanted them utilized, and he was opposed to forcing players to adopt a contrived format. Alleging he had done everything under the sun to convince the coach, he went to the owner.

Initially the fans were on Magic's case, disliking the audacity of labor holding management accountable. For the first and only time in his basketball life, Magic was booed. The owner recruited the team's radio commentator to be the interim coach, adding fuel to fan outrage. But the outrage was short lived as the Lakers won seventeen out of their next twenty games and went on to win the NBA championship. The coach who followed Magic's prescription was Pat Riley, who became one of the most

---

[1]See Chapter 16 of Culbert's *Mind-Set Management*.

respected and successful coaches in NBA history. And Magic's ball handling became art form and legend. No one playing before him recorded more career assists.

What Magic instinctively knew, and what we all need to remember, is that teamwork, effectively performed, is not a snap-together procedure. He displayed *inevitable subjectivity* awareness, essentially declaring that no set of expectations for someone's performance is realistic without first familiarizing yourself with how that individual sees the situation and what he or she can do best. And, he displayed *win-win-win politics*, insisting that no preconceived formula be superimposed on all players regardless of that person's competencies and limitations. Magic knew the team had to play in a manner that brought out the talents of each individual, including his own.

THE TWO-SIDED ACCOUNTABILITY APPROACH TO TEAMWORK

Launching into this new approach to teamwork requires some preparation once a group's goals are specified. The necessary next step, even prior to identifying methodologies and roles, should be a candid get-to-know-one-another discussion covering each person's personal stake in the project and preferred operating style. The purpose is to dispel two self-delusional, common misconceptions: (1) that others will conduct themselves rationally as you have reason to expect; (2) that it is safe to assume everyone is communicating effectively in the absence of your seeing a problem.

We're advocating a default assumption that no one sees or interprets events exactly as anyone else does. Thus the need and efficiency of spending up-front time finding out how others view situations and think become readily apparent. The range of topics should include what others see as their personal strengths and self-interested pursuits, preferences in roles and methodologies, types of situations each individual finds personally problematic, and forms of assistance and backup each will accept. For instance, some people don't like writing and tend to procrastinate when faced with a blank word processor screen. Knowing this in advance will not necessarily dictate a particular action, but it will suggest a perspective on how to approach an individual supportively when it appears that he or she could use some help.

The problem with snap-together teamwork is that performance problems almost always take team members by surprise and typically are followed by someone heavy-handedly invoking accountability that's one-sided. Usually this is done without sufficient up-front agreement about what expectations the deviating individual was supposed to meet or what the consequences would be for failing to do so. In the logic of two-sided accountability, one individual's failure to perform as expected should signal a group deficiency, not a single individual's fault. It alerts members to take stock of team resources and how they are being utilized. The reasoning is analogous to what two-sided accountability requires of hierarchical bosses: their accountability for taking stock of each subordinate's talents and positioning each person for success.

To view these differences, we've got a dynamite case showing that it's possible to get two-sided accountability institutionalized on a large scale. It's not a perfect application, but it's illustrative of much that we advocate and exemplifies how teamwork can be used to produce the type of growth and profitability every large company would like to realize. We encountered it in the late 1990s when corporate executives at The Home Depot asked us to review their management system for our impressions and candid thoughts.

The Home Depot Features Two-Sided Accountability Relationships and Teamwork

Desiring an outsider's opinion, executives of The Home Depot opened all their doors to us. We had access to every person in the management chain including board members and founding partners, then CEO Bernie Marcus and President Arthur Blank. We were encouraged to contact regional executives, store managers, and entry-level associates at any store, which is where we did most of our work.

Going in, we had few preconceptions other than doubts about ever seeing a large organization with institutionalized teamwork that was effective. Surprised by their effectiveness, we became engrossed in analyzing why. It became clear to us that two-sided accountability was the essential teamwork ingredient, but we also found pockets of activity in which hierarchical lowers experienced one-sided accountability. In every instance, these were areas with problems.

Background

To really appreciate what The Home Depot management is up to, imagine this situation: You need two screws to fix your washing machine. You go to a Home Depot store expecting to find the right ones, which you figure ought to set you back about forty cents. Entering the Goliath megastore, you follow the huge overhead banner signs to "hardware," requiring a ten-aisle hike to your right, then a hundred-foot trek toward the middle of the store. There you find a mind-boggling array of screws. Immediately you discover that you forgot screws come in different lengths, and you aren't sure of the screw length your washing machine requires. But screws are cheap, so you decide to load up on different lengths, reasoning that you'd gladly spend a couple of extra bucks to avoid a second trip.

Contemplating plausible sizes, you're approached by a sales associate who, unbeknownst to you, has observed your erratic search. Politely he asks, "What are you trying to fix?" You tell him, and he says, "Let's go over to our appliance center and see if we've got a washing machine like the one you're trying to fix. Maybe we can figure out what length you need."

The appliance center is several aisles over, and on the way you chat casually with this friendly guy who tells you that prior to hiring on at The Home Depot, he spent eighteen years as an electrician. Finding a washing machine that's similar to the one you have at home, you learn that all the screws you selected were the wrong variety. Moreover, the screws you need have an exotic head requiring a special wrench. The associate then takes you back to the screw aisle, picks out the correct ones, along with a wrench costing less than a dollar, and returns the screws you no longer need to their proper bins. You think, "Thank God for this guy. I would have bought all these wrong screws and maybe not gotten it right on the second trip." Heading for the checkout counter, you spot an outdoor lamp priced so cheaply you can't pass it up. You happily add the lamp to the two screws and small wrench in your shopping cart.

Driving home you think, "What's going on here? Hiring an electrician to help me purchase two screws is a far too expensive way to run a store." Right! The Home Depot's management is far more strategic. They have instructed the sales associate who helped you to think ahead. He has learned that a first time customer, treated well, can be expected over the course of a lifetime to spend more than $44,000 on purchases at The Home Depot. The screws and impulse purchase means that you only have $43,937.57 to go. And because the associate has worked for the company for over a year, he has a personal interest in your returning. Annually he receives stock options that, thanks to the loyalty of customers like you, are rapidly appreciating in value.

The Home Depot management aims to provide customer friendly, low-priced, one-stop shopping for all home improvement needs. This is the reason for making their stores so large. Managers and supervisors are instructed to treat all employees with the same focus and respect that they want employees to use with customers. In fact, executives want all employee interactions to be viewed as training activities, recognizing that their ambitious plan for doubling the number of locations every three and one-half to four years requires personnel "cloning." Each new store is staffed by a combination of experienced employees and new recruits whom management counts on to receive on-the-job training to the extent that they can become seed personnel for subsequent stores. And like the former electrician in our example, sales associates often are former tradespeople who are encouraged to advise customers on their home repair projects and recommend what they'll need.

Sales associates with "leadership" inclinations can move rapidly into store management and upward from there. Because each store's sales are so high, store management is considered a very responsible position, and The Home Depot pays people well for assuming it. We learned of store managers without high school diplomas who earn over $175,000 per year and of division and regional managers, without university degrees, earning considerably more. While acknowledging that their earnings are more than they ever expected to make, store managers also believe their pay is warranted based on the responsibilities they are given, their autonomy in running a store, and the many, many decisions they make bearing on their store's profitability. However, all is not what it seems to be.

Where Two-Sided Accountability Comes In

Each Home Depot store is a seemingly autonomous operating unit with department and store managers making most operational and business decisions. Conforming to what corporate has decided will be their basic product mix and which suppliers to use, department and store managers place their own orders. Suppliers ship directly to the store. Managers in departments such as paint, hardware, electrical, plumbing, garden, and lumber daily review computerized inventory printouts, hold meetings with sales associates to sense problems and assess new trends, order replenishments, create staffing plans, and publish weekly work schedules. Store managers review sales and profitability numbers and make all decisions, from choosing seasonal specials and placement of merchandise displays to hiring and promoting in-store personnel.

However, in our minds, the independence and autonomy implied by the activities and decision making authorities of in-store managers is far more illusory than real. The real intelligence and decision making is provided by a brilliantly thought out and comprehensive system of standards and variance controls that audit and constrain almost every decision an in-store manager makes. All purchasing, inventory, and staffing decisions are keyed into a computer that links to headquarters in Atlanta, providing instant feedback on their desirability prior to enactment. In a flash managers are alerted to suboptimal choices with statistics and graphs leading them toward the "right" reworked conclusion. For example, on Wednesday the paint department supervisor enters his staffing decisions for the coming week. The computer checks sales records to see how these choices compare with last week's volume and comparable periods and sales patterns in previous years. It also checks pricing specials, advertisements the company will run, industry trends, and even weather patterns that could affect product sales and store traffic. And it checks the availability of specific people, with adjustments made to accommodate individuals with family situations and part-time employees. In return, it sends the supervisor some precautionary messages and a set of graphs that can be used in iterating decisions. After a couple of adjustments, the supervisor hits on a pattern that the computer program deems close enough to optimal. The conclusions should not only be good for business but should result in bonus-level sales and significant augmentations in pay.

Should an individual fail to optimize, the computer sends a message that a problem exists. That results in a call from the district manager. In The Home Depot's managerial paradigm, the existence of a failure to optimize is not thought of as a glitch; it's considered a signal that an employee needs training.

One additional major feature of The Home Depot's store management must be understood in considering its application of two-sided accountability theory. The company protects itself and its employees by putting store management in a fishbowl.[2] All district and regional managers, and all executives regardless of specialty, "walk stores." Even board directors receive a quarterly quota of store locations to "walk." Store managers walk

---

[2] At the time of our study, The Home Depot had fewer than four hundred mega-sized stores nationwide. At this writing, it is on the brink of having one thousand, with a few stores in South America and expansion plans worldwide. For the last two years, our business with The Home Depot has been limited to that of customers, so we are unable to comment on current practices and structures.

their own stores daily and are assigned stores to walk in adjacent locales.

Walking a store is intended as a people check. It's seen as an opportunity to learn what sales associates are experiencing, a medium for on-the-spot training, and, most important, a moment to empathize with what associates are facing by building "we're on the same team together" relationships. Merchandise displays and aisle appearances are viewed as windows into how well personnel are trained and how well they perform assignments. When walking a store, a manager would never say, "Why is this aisle so dirty?" The protocol is to pick up a broom, sweep up the debris, and never say a thing.

Walks by corporate types and directors are typically followed up with meetings to give and receive feedback. Often these are impromptu with ad hoc groups of same-echelon people, without direct supervisors or managers present. Open-endedly a high-level person will inquire, "How's it *really* going?" At the time of our study, most employees felt they had a personal relationship with one or more "big bosses" and in some instances had a major boss's home telephone number. To cement a "family atmosphere," there are folksy newsletters, monthly team-building meetings held on closed-circuit television, and in-store information exchange meetings scheduled as needed.

We spent considerable time following store walkers and listening in on the conversations they held. We can personally vouch for the level of candor. Listening to gripes, some sounding quite well founded, the prototypical response was to offer advice that would allow the person with the problem to take constructive action on his or her own. All upper-level "walkers" offered backup assistance if the problem solvers' own efforts failed. It was commonplace for a walker to tell us that inside one specific complaint or another, he or she saw a system that needed updating or fixing.

MBA students who accompanied us found The Home Depot's approach to employees overly familial, gung-ho, and hokey for their "sophisticated" tastes. For example, regardless of which store we walked, we inevitably encountered sales associates who felt a personal relationship with Bernie Marcus or Arthur Blank. We listened to many sales associates tell stories about being hugged and even kissed by Bernie who, reportedly, was never at a loss to gush his appreciation for employee sacrifice and dedication. We witnessed department supervisors greeting arriving-to-work associates with "Thanks for coming in today." We were exposed to a retinue of stories about extreme adjustments in The Home Depot staffing pattern to accommodate someone "with a personal situation." And in every store we encountered pride in being associated with a firm that makes outstanding charitable and community service contributions. Taken as a package, what our students found overly patronizing seemed to be situationally appropriate management operating within a highly successful formula for producing people with a strong company identification, sense of camaraderie, and the kind of pride that translates into an incredible capacity to clone and train successful teams and managers.

We wondered whether associates having easy access to levels way above their boss would prove dangerous to lower- and middle-level managers. Would personality conflicts lead lowers with access to uppers to lodge unfounded criticisms and trumped-up complaints? What about the evaluation system used to rank associates? Would store proliferation and increasing numbers of people requiring evaluation lead to grading curves and pay enhancement quotas that turned off steady but unspectacular performers or create excessive competition within the ranks? The more we learned about The Home Depot's fish bowl system, the more questions popped up on our screen.

But the short answer to these questions and the others occurring to us is found in the positive tone we've been using in addressing this case. At the time of our study, The Home Depot checked out very, very well. Ready access to people at upper levels, the ever-present emphasis on training, the need for people to grow and advance into management of new stores, the strategy of building loyalty bonds with customers, and the complementary

building of loyalty bonds with employees through egalitarian relationships and share-the-wealth stock options are all significant
demonstrations of two-sided accountability.

For purposes of this book, there's little need to probe the management areas that we thought needed fixing. However, in the
spirit of balanced critique we'll mention one that was on our list.
At the time of our inquiry, we saw cultural confusion problems
emanating from some of the managers who had grown up in
working class homes and acquired their basic management
training as lead workers in a construction trade. When under
pressure or stressed, these managers struggled to override a
deep impulse to make straight-to-the-point, dictatorial statements that people on the receiving end would experience as
threatening and abusive. They groped to recall the nonhierarchical, human-sensitive approaches that The Home Depot
training had taught them. Nevertheless, taken as a package, we
saw The Home Depot system promoting candor and a very significant measure of reciprocal, two-sided accountability.

7

Top Levels Need to Support It

There's no question about it, two-sided accountability equates with organizational effectiveness. Thus, all the two-sided accountability efforts discussed so far have been on-point with a goal of improving company results. Conversely, we've repeatedly described how companies lose out when hierarchical relationships flourish. Self-delusion and corruption become overwhelming. What we haven't made explicit is our strong belief that people at the top must support two-sided accountability. This isn't to say that progress can't be made without them. But it is to say that it's an uphill climb without their sensitivity and support. Top-level people who insist on hierarchical relationships will straitjacket two-sided accountability efforts below. However inadvertently expressed, their one-sided demands will be a constant interruption to well-intentioned two-sided efforts and accomplishments.

The stunning open kimono illustration, the two-sided accountability case featured in Chapter 4, is a vivid case in point. After months of total intraproject cooperation, the deal was derailed when top dogs Mike Smith at Hughes and Craig McCaw at Teledesic went hierarchical with one another. Embroiled in a power struggle, each held out, futilely insisting that the other accept his "valid" view of what was needed to complete their deal. It took only a couple of head-butting, nonempathetic brief interactions for them to undo what more than five hundred professionals and executives had spent months achieving. From our vantage point, they were shameless in their disregard of what was being discarded. Each of their companies, as well as coprime Boeing and at least twenty subcontracting companies, lost tremendously in the process. With the deal's demise went a multisided accountability, business-partnering confederation of unprecedented potential.

Their falling out produced a wild and wooly aftermath. A behind-the-scenes deal was made to have Motorola replace Hughes and Boeing as prime contractor. Liking what they had seen in the open kimono partnering, Teledesic recruited as president and head of the Motorola deal the Hughes executive who had led that endeavor for them—which was fortunate for us, because it took only a couple of months for him to call for our assistance, asking us to make sure that the partnership worked well. That's the next accountability story we want to tell, and it's a doozey. It served to clarify further what true two-sided accountability entails and how easily people can be fooled when individuals steeped in a self-focused, hierarchical relationship mind-set use slogan words like *partnering* and *trusting relationships*, without knowing what it takes to make them substantive. Among other things it taught us the names of the four horsemen of the "Two-Sided Accountability Apocalypse," named for the qualities that undermine two-sided accountability. They are Insecurity, Self-indulgence, Narcissism, and Greed.

CASE 1

The Ease with Which Top-Level Executives Can Undermine Two-Sided Accountability Efforts Below

Teledesic and Motorola were in the fine-tuning stages of negotiating their multibillion-dollar contract that when signed, we were told, would become one of the biggest deals ever entered into by a coming out IPO. With such large sums at stake, the new president wanted the two companies aligned, with each committed to helping the other succeed. He wanted us briefed and immersed in the business plan, ready to begin at the final signing.

When getting briefed, we operate like investigative reporters. We interview well-placed people, soliciting their personal perspectives along with whatever factual information they can provide. In this case, we asked, "Tell us about your job in the Teledesic organization. How do you see the Teledesic/Motorola partnership, and what do you believe it's going to take to make this partnership effective?" We also mentioned our intent to proceed similarly at Motorola once the deal was signed.

In response to the "Tell us about your job" question, we heard too many people lacking clarity about roles, functions, and jurisdictions—their own as well as those of others. Multiple parties were performing similar functions. Adding confusion to overlap, people assuming similar functions reported to different executives. Some reported to the holding company's chairman, some to the company's CEO, and some to the company's president. Needless to say, their efforts were not coming together.

Sorting out jurisdictions was further complicated by a "culture of niceness" that prevented people from even surfacing their disputes. Nice to a fault, Teledesic personnel seemed to walk in fear of stepping on someone's toes and getting themselves labeled "difficult." The end result was that no one could get the authority to exercise what he or she had assumed was a role-related responsibility, and no one was held accountable for nonperformance because everyone could point to a high-level boss whose actions blocked their progress.

Adding to the problem were hierarchical relationships that also reeked of nonaccountability. For example, we heard about a contracting session in which the predecessor CEO asked the lead attorney to leave the room so he could confidentially hold a sensitive conversation with a lead Motorola executive. Afterward, in hushed tones, the CEO told the attorney about significant concessions made which the attorney assumed would be offset by gains in another venture. Six months later, when we interviewed him, the attorney still had not learned of an offsetting gain and was wondering whether the CEO had been duped. A one-sided accountability, hierarchical relationship had prevented the attorney from raising questions to check the soundness of the deal at the onset or follow-up questions later on. He feared a negative response.

Two blatant and important findings emerged from our interviews. First, the Teledesic people we interviewed perceived their company's motives and requirements to be quite different from those they attributed to Motorola. Second, in one form or another, each depicted Teledesic as not having its internal "act" together.

Both conclusions led us to the very top: the company's third CEO in three years and the newly recruited president. Our interviews had us convinced that Teledesic's top executives were mired in jurisdictional dilemmas and overlapping functions comparable to what the ranks below needed resolved. We could see no way of overcoming internal disorganization until these two executives clarified territory and roles. Encouraging them to differentiate, and helping them do so, became the second step of our consultation. Step 1 was giving them an overall report of what we thought the company needed to confront in readying itself for Motorola.

Ironically, we recommended that when referring to interactions with Motorola, Teledesic personnel not use the term *partnering*. Meeting with the CEO and the president, we explained, "Using this term will be disorienting and may eventually evoke feelings of disappointment and betrayal." When they asked, "Why?" we responded, "Because the term *partnering* creates expectations that you are on a common track, looking out for one another's interests. This does not depict how Teledesic personnel see Motorola executives behaving.

We explained, "Looking through the eyes of your key legal, technical, and financial people, we get a picture of two companies driven by different forces. You and your guys are looking for a high-capacity, state-of-the-art technical system with customer-friendly equipment in a venture that you see as financially risky, given that Teledesic and its investors lose out completely if the end system doesn't perform as promised. In contrast, your people see Motorola as trying to rescue a technology it developed years ago, which your experts claim has yet to be successfully deployed, with a contract that provides them high-margin payments for reaching manufacturing milestones that can't be evaluated until the entire system is complete. Furthermore, the cultures sound quite different. Your guys make Motorola sound interpersonally aggressive, with people fearing for their careers when differing with a boss. They perceive rigidity in the way Motorola's technical people operate, an inability to shift course to take the 'right' action when under the belief that their boss wants something else. This differs from your guys, who are confused about lines of authority to the point that they readily shift direction without consulting a boss and behave as if they would lose territory and power by streamlining and eliminating duplication."

Cutting to the chase, we took up our second point, which, in our minds, was where they needed to start. We told them, "Despite your outwardly friendly appearances, we don't see the two of you working well together. There does seem to be an abundance of leadership work that needs accomplishing, more than enough for the two of you, but it's not getting done. We don't see either of you lacking positive motivation. Rather, we think you've got the same problem as the people in the ranks below you. Your boss has failed to stipulate clearly precisely what functions you, and you alone, perform." Going into more detail we said, "Perhaps the two of you should call on your chairman together and ask him to delineate who has what responsibility and authority while the three of you are in the same room. Alternatively, maybe you can sort it out yourselves." Each of them preferred the latter. We made an early-next-morning date to differentiate jurisdictions.

That discussion was amazingly brief and tension-free to the point that, in an effort to confront them with our disbelief, we called it a "love-in." Contrasting the job descriptions received from the chairman revealed almost total overlap. Intimidated by their culture's imperative to appear nice and not wanting to lose territory, they, too, had lacked the means to reconcile their duplication. They discussed why they repeatedly clashed and how people to whom they gave conflicting instructions felt forced to go see the chairman. They also saw how the chairman undermined their authorities by not making definitive clarifications.

Realizing that they had good cause for stepping on one another's territory, that they lacked the authority to exercise their role responsibilities, and that their conflict over responsibilities had the effect of ceding all their power to the chairman paved the way to agreement. Quickly they differentiated roles in a way that paralleled convention. That differentiation called for the president to lead the internal operations and the CEO to lead external. However, since neither liked the idea of being pigeonholed, they agreed to lead jointly all planning activities and to consult one another on any decision that set or impacted policy.

Meeting again two weeks later, we found them out of sorts with one another. Each cited ways in which the other had "violated" their new agreement. This led to their writing down a very explicit and highly articulated statement of jurisdictions and functions for each that the other promised to respect. To embed these agreements and reorient senior staff, they called a meeting to present and discuss their plan. Circulating a statement of differentiated job functions, they promised to produce an organization chart that would do the same for senior staff. Then there would be meetings and discussions to redo the organization chart so that functional systems would integrate.

To our surprise, senior staff reacted with such low energy that we later referenced their reaction as "a group yawn." Incredulous, we asked, "Why aren't you more enthusiastic? Isn't this exactly what you told us the company needed?" They responded with variations of "We've heard this one before from each previous president and CEO." Senior staff's taking a "we'll believe it when we see it" attitude gave the CEO and president a clear line of sight on their common fate. Preserving their credibility became an additional motivation for making their relationship work.

There's a postscript to this story that supports our initial point in spades about Teledesic not having its internal act together. While the president was organizing and streamlining operations and the

CEO aggregating direct reports, the chairman pulled the plug on their partnership. He fired the president and redeployed the CEO. Our immediate reaction was to think the chairman saw their plan to reorganize depriving him of a central role in daily operations. Based on what we subsequently learned, it's likely his motivations also included not wanting anyone beside himself positioned to adjust parameters of the deal with Motorola. Six months later, stationed as outside onlookers, the Teledesic project and the company's "partnership" with Motorola appeared inert. A year and a half after that, it dissolved. In a culture shaped by high-level hierarchical relationships, no one was left with enough job security either to give the company direction or to call the chairman to account for actions that, unexplained, served to feed demoralization and cynicism. Once again the company appeared to be in a state of wheel-spinning, animated suspension. Informally we heard many accounts of fed up staff feeling stuck, unable to quit without giving up the rights to IPO options they were counting on to eventually make them wealthy.

WHO OWNS THE COMPANY, ANYWAY?

Working with top-level executives of publicly held companies, along with start-up operations like Teledesic, and talking with some of the people who sit on their boards has caused us to question which stakeholder interests are in the forefront of executives' minds when making the big-buck decisions that direct the company. Of course, all of them recite the holy mantra "We're here to create shareholder value," and they speak it in heavenly tones. But when shareholders like the two of us look in the mirror, we don't see any one ethereal. We don't even see "shareholders;" we merely see "speculators." There's not a security we wouldn't dump in a moment if we thought the share price was about to drop. We've even got shares in companies that we know nothing about, including what business the company is in, bought on the say-so of someone we trust. Moreover, when we look at some of the pay deals these executives have cut for themselves, at their self-indulgent excesses such as calling nonessential meetings that interrupt the productive routines of tens and scores of people, and at their living luxuriously on the corporate expense account and buying expensive jets, we don't get the impression that these people actually lose sleep worrying about shareholders. If they're not primarily looking out for their "shareholders," then whose interests are they looking out for?

Confronting them with our irreverence, we challenge top-level executives to tell us "the truth." When they reiterate that their decisions are being made on the criterion of "maximizing shareholder interests," we challenge them to provide the name of one widow or orphan whose well-being is primary on their minds. We go so far as to ask them their feelings about the mutual funds that, on a quarterly basis, mau-mau them for additional pennies in quarterly profits.

Pushed to the wall, executives name "employees and customers" as the people whose interests they work for. But examining the actual decisions they make and the thinking behind them, their assertions seldom strike us as credible. For example, consider the response Mike Smith, CEO of General Motors, Hughes, gave to an engineer during a closed-circuit TV Q and A session held to explain the sale of the company's Space and Communications Division to Boeing. Aghast at the prospects of going to work for a former competitor, whose management Hughes's executives had for years maligned and derided, the engineer inquired, "Once you decided to sell the company, didn't you have any offers from better-managed firms?" Appearing noticeably irritated, Mike Smith revealed what we thought to be his underlying thinking. In essence, he responded with the old love-it-or-leave-it line "If you don't like it, go get a job somewhere else," as if the engineer's self-interested concerns were without foundation and as if his well-being wasn't affected by this sale. Of course, as the holder of hundreds of thousands of options of a stock that jumped up dramatically upon rumor of the sale, and jumped up again on the public announcement of the $3.75 billion deal, Mike Smith's shareholders seemed to come out quite well.

To us Mike Smith's alleged answer was telling, not just about how executives at General Motors, Hughes think, but also about how many top-level executives reason. Fearing that the people they count on for execution will get the "wrong impression," executives take care to keep their wealth accumulation desires sufficiently hidden not to render their decisions suspect. In contrast, the start-up dot-com companies seem to have found the answer. They finesse the issue of the boss's accumulation of wealth by awarding ownership options to every key employee. On the come, highly talented and creative people receiving average salaries willingly work twelve or more hours a day, six and seven days a week, believing that eventually the company will go public and their conversions of options to stock will make them rich. If ever there were a group of people whose "over and above the call of duty" ownership contributions entitled them to hold their bosses accountable, it's these start-up employees. But do they?

We know of no sizeable organization in which start-up people below the uppermost echelon, option holders working extraordinary hours, have established a nondismissible measure of reciprocal accountability with their bosses. We even can be quite specific about the mind-set that would produce it. In fact, it's the same mind-set we think people in established companies, who have earn-as-you-work jobs, should have employed long ago. People in the ranks need to see being the boss as just another job. When they do, they will insist that their executives *join the company team* by behaving as two-sided accountability leaders.

It's ironic, since this is what just about every executive we've ever heard of contends he or she is doing in every company speech they make. Publicly they claim that being boss and leader is merely performing another job that needs to be done. But we don't see many bosses acting as if they know the first thing about how they might behave differently if they were to take their own words literally.

Two-Sided Accountability Leadership Entails Setting Precedent

Whether we're talking the high or low end of the totem pole, everyone in a company has the same mandate: perform competently and team-contribute by supporting and facilitating the competent performances of others. This is the team-play mind-set. It's what everyone in a company should be committed to enact. This is what uppers to the boss think; it's what lowers are expected to think; it's how bosses need to think; and, more important, it's how they need to behave.

Several factors prevent bosses from acting as two-sides-accountable team players. We've already covered two: self-delusion and personal ego. In the next chapter we'll add several others and describe our recommendation for the system fix. And it's not just overly self-involved bosses who fail to join the team. Failing to join are many bosses with exemplary motivations who lack the team-play mind-set for the functions a boss needs to fulfill. Up front we can tell you that the punch line for how these functions should be performed is the same. It's the boss practicing two-sided accountability. What would be different if a boss actually practiced two-sided accountability? What actions would signify his or her commitment to team play?

Now we're going to get concrete. We're going to step beyond the transformations described in Chapters 3 and 4, and beyond the two-sided accountability principles lined up in Chapter 5, to suggest some tangible steps to be taken by executives and bosses who desire a culture in which two-sided accountability relationships flourish. These steps are not substitutes for internalizing the principles of two-sided accountability, with *inevitable subjectivity* and *win-win-win* political reasoning. They are logical extensions.

What's Required for Two-Sided Accountability Leadership?

1. Getting Informed Top of the list for the boss who wants to lead the changeover to two-sides-accountable partnering is getting adequately briefed and informed prior to making important decisions. Bosses practicing one-sided accountability will assert that they already do this. In good leadership tradition, they hold meetings, listen to presentations, read reports, consult experts, and generally do their homework.

But bosses who practice two-sided accountability do substantially more. They open their decisions to review and stand accountable.

After getting briefed and performing relevant reconnaissance, but prior to finalizing their decisions and taking decisive action, they put their preliminary conclusions on the table for critique by knowledgeable people they trust. Practicing two-sided accountability they explain their thinking, answer questions, and open-mindedly engage alternative proposals and counter arguments. Only after their thinking is vetted, and modifications considered appropriate are made, do they act.

This gives sounding-board advisers who believe differently the opportunity to challenge the boss's thinking. Of course at the end of the day, the boss will act as he or she sees fit. That goes with the authority. And because it's judgment, not secret information, that determines the boss's actions, decisions can be tracked against outcomes and, where necessary, revised. Accountability is two-sided because the boss can't hide behind the old "If you knew what I know that I am not at liberty to divulge to you, then you would have acted as I did" excuse. The result should be more trust and confidence from the people working with them who, because of the boss's openness, are likely to reciprocate with more openness of their own. In the end, the company benefits from the thinking of more of the people inside it.

2. Informing Others Next on the list for bosses engaging in team play is getting subordinates the information required for them to perform their jobs competently. Once again, bosses who practice one-sided accountability will say they already do this based on the front-end information sharing and perspective-setting discussions they hold when assigning a project or responsibility. Their beliefs are reinforced by the information updates they provide and the midcourse corrections they advance. But from where we sit, the aforementioned schema is more tactical than strategic. It leads to experiences like the one related to us by the attorney who wondered whether his CEO had been duped, described in the opening case in this chapter.

Practicing two-sided accountability entails giving subordinates a strategic perspective on their assignments and sufficient information about what's expected in the way of results. To be strategic, subordinates need to be present when a project need is formulated or at least when key parameters for the project are initially discussed and mapped. To be strategic, oversight involves a roll-up your sleeves work session, not just a "Can you find the holes in how we've been going about this?" presentation. To be strategic, the boss takes the role of learning what subordinates require to "get it right," not just evaluating whether they have it "right," the way he or she wants it done. The Chapter 2 case of the MBA who wanted to star clearly illustrates the type of involvement needed here. Recall how we saw her faced with the unnerving situation of having her bosses withhold perspectives for fear of biasing her conclusions. Their action would keep her off balance, and the company would lack the means for getting her best.

When there's two-sided accountability, the boss's involvement doesn't stop with making sure that subordinates have the information he or she thinks is needed. It includes finding out what information subordinates want and helping them access it. With two-sided accountability, subordinates are accountable for producing results while bosses are accountable for making sure subordinates have what they need to produce *great* results.

3. Conserve Human Capital Next on our list is the boss's utilization of human capital. Here the differences between bosses who practice one-sided and two-sided accountability are particularly obvious. One-side-accountable bosses are wasteful of other people's time. They engage in self-indulgent acts like the CEO's speech that wasted fifteen minutes of a thousand people's time, described in Chapter 2. They schedule meetings without giving serious consideration to lowers who can't insist on a more convenient time. They automatically assume meetings to be at their office location regardless of the number of people who must transport themselves there. They have canned apologies for people they leave waiting in their outer office for an hour or more, rereading the previous day's *Wall Street Journal*. They assign projects that are considered wasted efforts by the people performing them, ignoring their complaints of futility. The list of human effort wasted and opportunities lost is endless.

On the other hand, bosses who practice two-sided accountability are seriously interested in subordinate productivity. They align their self-interests with the total corporate effort by measuring efficiency and productivity in terms of total team progress and company results, making these their ego-gratifying accomplishments. They inquire about availability prior to making an assignment; they solicit the other person's viewpoint with a concern for conserving effort. When invoking urgency, they consider off-loading other number one priorities. They display an active interest in each individual's well-being and morale. In short, they produce asset value by fostering personally rewarding, productive relationships between personnel and company efforts.

4. Engage People Personally The last item on our boss-as-leader functions is knowledge of the needs of other people and acceptance of one's role in facilitating their pursuits. We're not just talking about what people lower down need to perform their assignments competently; we're talking about what drives them personally, professionally, and corporately—what they must realize to make their company affiliation personally meaningful. This is the "if you're going to be a leader, you need to know what the people you are leading think" mind-set that everyone in a leadership position acknowledges. It's another way of putting *inevitable subjectivity* and *win-win-win politics* together, finding out what you need to know to grasp another's perspective and gain his or her enthusiastic participation by seeking outcomes consistent not only with your interests and the company's but with the other person's also.

Aware of the value of knowing what's on the minds of people below them and how they see organizational events, big bosses sponsor an endless stream of activities. These include hosting informal brown bag lunches for interactive discussions, holding periodic open forums for discussion of controversial topics, encouraging direct reports to submit agenda topics for team meetings, regularly scheduling one-on-one supervisory meetings, conducting anonymous surveys, and receiving 360-degree feedback conducted by third parties, with new modalities on the drawing boards.

Unfortunately, most of these activities are carried on with one-sided accountability. Brown bag sessions intended to be responsive to employee concerns turn into sales sessions in which giving the company line supplants listening to how other people see it, as in the aforementioned Mike Smith vignette. Topics nominated for management meetings get the "back of the line" treatment as the executive in charge arranges the agenda to ensure that his or her urgent issue is taken up prior to time running out. One-on-one meetings are kept only when the boss has something to discuss. Human Resources takes control of the open forums and uses them to explain proposed changes in benefits and parking. Anonymous surveys are engaged defensively as recipients react as if the objective is to clean up the list rather than hold focused discussion to engage and explain. Three hundred sixty–degree feedback is helpful in belling the cat but not in changing underlying beliefs or developing relationships. The reaction is vivid: people stop participating. They protect themselves by quickly adopting a "been there, done that" attitude when hearing the coming attractions.

Two-sided accountability changes all this. It is face-to-face, not anonymous, with initial discussions on the topic of "To speak candidly, what do you need from me?" Recall that two-sided accountability incorporates the inevitable subjectivity principle and the fact that underlying each person's company affiliation are desires to pursue life needs, maximize rewards and gains, and receive good value for sacrifices made. The boss's listening and learning is emphasized. Any meeting in which the boss does lots of talking is followed up with meetings devoted to inquiring, "What did you hear and where did you come out?" Two-sided accountability requires the boss to work on developing a capacity to live with tension and differences that aren't reconciled. The modus operandus is power sharing, not power taking where the boss unilaterally frames the issue. Neither is it power denying, where the boss uses the uniqueness of a subordinate's concern to discredit that individual's position.

CONCLUSION

This chapter explains how the accountability mind-set of people at the very top impacts the capacities of people lower down to achieve two-sided accountability relationships. Failure to adopt two-sided accountability sets big bosses apart from the people in their company, a distance that breeds additional hierarchical relationships. Keep in mind that it's not just the careless and self-indulgent who are one-sided in their functioning; it's also some very well-intentioned executives who champion teamwork and empowerment and who have read the books and taken the courses. Even people who genuinely want their subordinates to perform well and are willing to give credit where it is due are clueless about what two-sided accountability leadership actually entails. In their minds they're doing it right. Because of this mind-set, they don't receive behavioral messages that signal the contrary. They fail to understand that it's hierarchical relationships that are screwing things up. They're so immersed in the one-sided accountability paradigm that they don't see the two-sided alternative.

Bosses who truly want to act as leaders need to bring two-sided accountability to their roles. The next chapter presents a radical proposal for setting in motion the political dynamics that might just succeed in doing so.

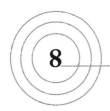

8

Changing the Structure to Encourage It

For some time we've been walking around with a back-pocket proposal for promoting two-sided accountability relationships. It's for a management structure that can produce the types of experiences that cause mind-sets to transform. Unfortunately, it's a proposal that initially makes people accustomed to hierarchical relationships quiver, squirm, and flinch. Because of this, we try not to expose our proposal to executives we haven't had a chance to soften up. Sometimes we present it after a slide show where, using disconcerting questions like those in Chapter 3, we demonstrate how people readily overlook principles of human conduct in their daily dealings at work. Sometimes we present our proposal after a dramatic consulting episode in which we assist people who interact competitively to recognize their common interests and partner up. Sometimes it's after a round of golf with a managerial leader. Blue-skying it on the nineteenth hole, playing to a manager's relaxed state and open-mindedness, we let our proposal out.

But even softened up, managers accustomed to hierarchical relationships are thrown by what we suggest. While we intend to have our proposal taken literally, most respond as if we've made a joke. When we reiterate to emphasize that we're dead serious, many continue "south." Instead of wrapping their minds around opportunities for applying what we're suggesting and what their company might gain, they get stuck focusing on what they initially see as impractical. Why all the resistance and negativity? We think it's because our proposal appears to limit a manager's ability to operate with command-and-control authority in ways most people haven't considered feasible. No doubt another reason is that our proposal threatens to create a continuous stream of actual managerial work.

Now we're going to take on the most difficult assignment we have faced in writing this book. We're going to pitch you the very proposal that many people ardently resist. However, before presenting it, we want to give you some points of reference so you can see where we're coming from and where we're trying to get. At a minimum, you'll find these reference points useful should you attempt to implement aspects of what we are about to suggest.

REFERENCE POINT 1:
When Do People Get Most Turned On at Work?

Take a moment to reflect about the work experiences that professionals, managers, and newcomer executives most often cite when asked to describe the most enjoyable, rewarding, and empowered moments they've experienced at work. What would you say they were? When do people feel the best about what they are doing and, perhaps because of this, believe they are performing at their best?

While the specifics are always different, the majority of people we query cite situations in which they had an important responsibility, the authority to exercise it, and top-level decision makers depending on them for direction and results. Analyzing specifics, we often find references to participation on a multidisciplined and time-bounded project team, one that operated without hierarchy and without anyone's direct boss in the vicinity.

It's worthwhile to notice that most project teams are composed of like-echelon people working together as peers. In instances where some upper-echelon people are on the team, they are treated as equals without distinction for hierarchical rank or senior status role. Usually team leadership is fluid and traded around.

Generally the leader's role is to coordinate and make sure all "bases" are covered and circumscribed to limit the impression that any one person is singularly responsible for any particular result. While team members make sincere efforts to compliment teammates for exceptional contributions, recipients almost always dismiss personal accolades as unwarranted. And to some extent they're correct.

Even people who believe their efforts are outstanding see the autonomy and confidence extended to them by teammates as the essential stage setter. Because of this, they don't think of themselves as making separable contributions; they sincerely think of themselves as part of a team effort. And that's how the effort is judged. When results fall below the quality expected, it's far more common to hear people say, "We gave it an honest effort, learned a great deal, and will do substantially better next time" than to say, "We would have been successful if some of our guys hadn't screwed up."

Generally, the individual commissioning a project team is located an echelon or more above the level of each team member's boss. Usually it's this "big boss" who frames the problem, declares what value the project has to the company, and whose opinion matters most in evaluating what's accomplished.

Unintended as it might be, we think this individual's two echelon or more distance from where the people on the team fit on the organization chart is instrumental to the group's productivity. It moves team members out of a direct reporting line, replacing the intimidation of one-sided accountability with two-sided, give-and-take accountability toward other team members. The result is that each person on the team thinks straighter, talks straighter, exchanges feedback more freely, and is more open to questioning and examining novel ideas. Team members are less prone to defending, less fearful of taking risks, and more assertive in accessing individuals with whom they feel the need to speak, regardless of hierarchical level. Vicariously they operate as if they had the backing of the person at the top, although they seldom ask the top-level boss to intervene on their behalf. Of course, each individual can always consult his or her direct boss—and does for technical direction. But it is only under extraordinary circumstances that an individual feels pressured by what his or her direct boss wants or feels compelled to pursue a direction that differs from what he or she personally believes best.

REFERENCE POINT 2:
Strong Leaders Have Difficulty Getting Leadership from the Ranks

We frequently hear executives with "strong leader" reputations complain about not getting enough leadership from levels below. In fact, just recently we encountered this complaint from the entrepreneur founder of a rapidly growing client services company. Five years from retirement, he was puzzling whether to create an employee stock ownership plan (ESOP) or sell his company to a larger firm. He said he preferred selling to loyal employees, many of whom have been with him ten to twenty years. He also said he felt an obligation to customers he feared would not receive the same focus and high-quality treatment if the company became a larger firm's subsidiary. The problem is, he told us, "I'm not sure which of my executives to groom to be my successor."

After several visits to learn his business and acquaint ourselves with his executives, we engaged him in serious conversation. Closing his office door, we began, "Frankly, we don't hear about anyone besides you taking the lead on important company initiatives. You also seem to be the only one who lies awake all night worrying about problems and taking total responsibility for getting them solved. We've made a point of asking each of your direct reports why they take so long putting key initiatives from their domains into operation. To us, their actions lack urgency. Are we seeing things differently than you do?"

He responded thoughtfully, "I've seen it this way for a while. It's just that I found it too painful to verbalize." Continuing, he gave us a "personal constitution" explanation for what we had noticed. This leader saw himself having the personal constitution to lead and was wondering whether the others lacked it. Then, anticipating what he thought we'd say, he commented, "And I don't want to hear any goddamn explanation for how I'm creating dependent people and have to change my ways. If these people had the right mettle, it wouldn't make any difference what I was doing. It takes far less to get through to me than any other boss they'll get."

We asked, "Would you mind our sharing *our* observation with some of your direct reports? We'd like to get their reactions." He shook his head affirmatively, saying, "I have no objections at all, not a damn one!"

We're sure just about every reader anticipates what we heard, for this is an archetypal problem in strong-leader, autocratically run companies. Each direct report agreed with our observation, and several commented, "And this problem is getting worse." And none saw their own leadership capabilities as the problem. Instead, each told stories describing actions they didn't take because they believed this leader would disapprove.

Reporting back, we told him, "They agree with our observation that no one besides you initiates much leadership. And, as you might suspect, they don't see themselves lacking leadership capabilities. Their goals mirror yours; they would like to step up to take on real leadership. As a remedy, we recommend a three- to four-hour time block for the leadership team to sit down with us to review and redesign a plan for dispersing leadership authorities. The emphasis should be less on why you guys are in this situation and more on a plan for breaking out," we told him. Intentionally, we omitted a search for the "why?" We feared doing so would get us into psychodynamics and further leadership bog-down. Later on, when there was time, we would probe other factors more forthrightly.

The leader's response to our "leadership initiative" became, for us, a case in point. Instead of running with our proposal, he unilaterally suspended communications. First, our e-mail and telephone request for a meeting date went unanswered. Then, when we called to inquire what was going on, he told us he was interviewing each of the people with whom we had spoken to see "what they truly thought" and whether they were in agreement with our proposal to hold a group discussion. He told us, "I'll be getting back to you just as soon as I think through where I'm 'coming out.'" "Hey," we thought, "we were trying to lead this initiative." The implications were clear. He wanted us to sit back and wait for him to lead.

Because our client was the top boss, there was no one to whom we could appeal in bringing additional open-mindedness to our situation. We didn't see this leader doing anything "wrong"; we saw him just doing "his thing," which, in this instance, was blocking our way of dealing with the problem he had commissioned us to address. If he didn't have a "thing," he wouldn't have asked for our help. We all have "things." That's another good aspect of hierarchy. Having a bigger boss to bring into a conversation can be a relationship leveler. So we were blocked, feeling just like the people he criticized. However, unlike full-time employees, we could bet the relationship. Without getting into the details, we called him to assert, "Come on! This is our domain of expertise. Aren't you going to allow us to lead our initiative?" The implication was transparent. We had his attention. Finally, he came around.

REFERENCE POINT 3:
When Do People Want Their Boss in the Room While Holding an Important Candid Conversation with Their Boss's Boss?

Some subordinate/boss relationships are so close and trustworthy that having one's boss present in a conversation with the boss's boss, the "big boss," is never a problem. But, in the vast majority of cases, notwithstanding the political motive to appear loyal at all times, the standard answer to this question is "seldom to never."

Consider the differences, particularly in light of the intimidation and corruption that frequents hierarchical relationships.

Imagine the different types of conversations that take place when the direct boss is present and when he or she is absent. In fact, we've got a situation at our fingertips involving a high-potential executive named Mel. Actually, this case illustrates several reference points, so we're going to run it as a miniserialization.

> ### Serialized Case: "The Leader Who Was Too Smart," Part I
>
> Mel became incensed when his direct boss, the COO, gave him a bigger job and then reneged on a promise to make him a vice president. Instead, he was given a car and more money and options, and he was told the VP title would be forthcoming. When Mel asked why the delay, the COO said it was merely a formality. Mel then asked to see the company's president. He wanted to learn what was actually taking place to determine whether the title was in fact an eventuality. "Let me know if it's an indefinite 'put-off,'" Mel told the president "so I can begin looking for another job."
>
> The president told Mel that his former peers, who would become his direct reports, were afraid of him and needed some time to adjust to the change in relationships. Mel balked, saying, "How am I going to do this job without the authority to direct?" As a compromise, the president offered, "I'll make sure that each of them knows your opinion will bear heavily on their reviews and bonuses." Then, as we got it from Mel, the president went on to emphasize how much he needed Mel in this oversight role due to losing confidence in the COO.
>
> Mel had been in the bigger job two months when we got the call from the COO, Mel's boss, to provide Mel some management coaching. Apparently, the former peers, now "subordinates," were still complaining. But they weren't complaining to Mel.

Are you surprised that Mel's newly deemed subordinates didn't take their discomforts directly to Mel, preferring to take their complaints to his boss, their former boss and new big boss? Are you surprised that Mel had to go to his big boss, the company president, to get a message that his direct boss, the COO, should have delivered? Are you surprised that he didn't go until his doubts about whether he'd ever get the vice president title reached a crescendo level? We don't think any organizational veteran would find any of these actions surprising. Fear of reprisal, competitive urges, disbelief that the other party in a boss/subordinate relationship will exercise "objectivity"—all make it difficult to broach managerial problems such as these.

Minisummary

So far we've covered three reference points. First, people in self-directed work teams are turned on by working on high-visibility projects with the authority to do what they think is correct, without hierarchical meddling by a direct boss. Second, bosses who complain about not getting leadership from the ranks often don't realize the extent to which their one-sided accountability, hierarchical styles stifle leadership from below. Third, big bosses are sought as righting mechanisms by subordinates who experience their direct boss behaving competitively with them. We've got three more reference points to go. When you line up these six points, they take you directly to the logic of our proposal.

REFERENCE POINT 4:
The Higher Up You Look, the Fewer Real Managers You Find

It's been about twenty-five years since the call went out for a prestige and pay progression track for high-functioning technical people that would parallel the stature and remuneration managers progressing upward on the organization chart received. Until then, the only way to reward a valuable technical contributor was through promotion up the managerial ranks. It also had been thought that giving technically clever individuals more people to direct would leverage and amplify their contributions. But mismanagement errors and people complaints overturned this thinking.

Recognizing that technical smarts didn't always translate to smarts in managing people, human resource experts began to search for alternatives. New high-level staff positions were created with technical titles to designate that these "brainy" people were expert problem solvers and advisers, not line managers. Creating high-level technical staff positions allowed management to pay them more and avoid blatant inequities. Unfortunately, not all of these people got out of the managerial chain. When downsizing hit, their reputations as inadequate managers made them immediately expendable.

However, the problem is back. This time it's in the executive ranks. The organization chart is stacked with executives who, at a point in time, might have been able enough overseers of individuals but whose high-level operative roles preclude any serious management activity. These executives solve problems, make decisions, cut deals, interact and negotiate with outsiders, and generally perform most of the company's high-visibility roles. Time consuming, behind the scenes cultivating of and caring for people is no match for the immediate gratification, glamour, and excitement that they receive from limelight roles. What little staging for other people's effectiveness they perform is often no more than crisis management of a malfunctioning individual or a reaction to a direct report threatening to leave.

Needed are executives who have the time to manage people, and here we're talking "macromanaging" not "micro." *Macro* means listening and getting into an individual's logic to better understand how he or she thinks and reasons. It means giving advice only after you've heard that individual out and considered how to frame your advice to be contextually relevant to his or her concerns and needs. In contrast, micromanaging entails giving instructions and directions without serious regard for how the other person sees events that create the need for your advice. The core objective of macromanaging is the boss's learning. In micro, it's instructing a subordinate to do what the boss believes is right.

In our experience, the problem we're citing is most blatant and visible at the top where people reporting to top-most executives are seasoned veterans who require macro guidance, not instrumental instruction. But most top executives behave as if communicating what they have to say is far more important and efficient than listening and guiding. On this they are dead wrong. People in general—top-level direct reports, especially—are far more inclined to internalize lessons they uncover themselves than to follow directives they receive from a boss. It's the old "Don't tell me, Dad—let me figure this out for myself" phenomenon. In fact, they often experience a boss's problem solving and advice as competitive with the credit they would like to receive, even when the boss is dead-on correct. For a graphic illustration, we return to the serialized story of Mel.

Serialized Case: "The Leader Who Was Too Smart," Part II

We'd have to rank coaching Mel among the most gratifying consulting assignments we've ever had. Even though it was Mel's boss who called us in, he did so because we were Mel's choice. Of course, our first step was an in-depth conversation with Mel. We needed to learn his personal background, his beliefs about people, and what he saw as his new role in managing a group of former peers, business unit leaders, and engineers, who had raised objections to his being made their boss. When we asked Mel what reason people might have for being afraid of him, Mel was nonplused. He couldn't imagine why. At this point he got a bit worked up wondering why no complainer had come to him to express a problem or misgiving.

Ending the interview, we told Mel that we'd like to get the impressions of work associates, uppers, peers, and subordinates who knew him well. We asked him to make a list, encouraging him to include people he guessed had complained about his becoming their line boss. Seeing himself bum-rapped, Mel liked the idea of our accessing their views. We asked him to e-mail people on his list explaining that he had contracted for some management coaching and would appreciate a candid sharing of their thoughts.

Introducing ourselves as Mel's management coaches, we explained that our job was to assist Mel to become "an even better

manager" than he already was. We explained, "The objective of
this discussion is simply for you to make us smarter about Mel."
Promising anonymity, we told "prospective informants" that we
would take pains not to divulge anything specific that could link
them with advice we gave Mel. We said we would personally
own every impression we conveyed. By the third interview, we
were confident that we understood what caused his former peers
to fear him. Mel could outsmart them at every turn.

We learned that Mel was one of those extraordinary people who
appears remote and doodles when knotty problems are being
discussed when, in fact, he's totally engrossed trying to figure
out a solution. Moreover, Mel's solutions seldom resembled anyone else's. Apparently Mel used a different, more powerful paradigm that produced answers that weren't readily available in
more conventional ways of formulating problems. Too many
times people had the experience of watching Mel, in a matter of
minutes, figure out solutions to critical problems that for
months had perplexed entire work units. Silently Mel would re-
frame the problem into a format where he could see a solution.
But Mel didn't reveal how he framed the problem; he merely
presented his solution. From Mel we got the impression he
didn't realize that others failed to comprehend his unconventional formulations.

Counseling Mel, we said, "You need to recognize that your job
has changed. Prior to taking on this new executive function,
everyone who is now scheduled to report to you was your peer.
In that context they could control your access to their problems
and, only at moments of desperation, allow you to see a problem
that they knew you could figure out and solve. They subcon-
sciously limited your access because they didn't want to feel up-
staged. They now fear that as boss you will have hierarchical
access to all of their knotty problems and that your problem
solving will make them appear incompetent. But as vice president your job is not to solve problems. Your job is to stage for
others to solve problems so that they can be seen as effective.
And when you think about what you do to solve problems, this
should be relatively easy. Draw out the person with the problem,

share your different frame, and step back while the new framework takes them to solutions they couldn't previously envision. Then instead of their seeing you as a competitor, they'll see you as a problem-solving ally. When they find themselves better off for having you around, they'll become staunch supporters. That's human nature."

This turned out to be a managerial Cinderella story. With only a few reminders, Mel changed his managerial approach. Three months later he was made vice president. Less than six months after that, two unit heads retired and the company was reorganized to create an expanded senior vice president and COO role, with Mel's old boss moved to special assignment. No one was surprised—nor was an objection raised—when the jungle tom-toms spread the rumor about what would be Mel's next role.

This story portrays a behavioral dynamic that's prevalent in organizations today, particularly in high-tech and dot-com companies. People high up in the hierarchy love to make decisions and problem-solve. What leaders fail to recognize is how competitively subordinates experience such actions. If we've said it once, we've said it thousands of times when coaching executives: "Above all else, managing and leading entail establishing the conditions for *other people to succeed.*" Now we should take this a step further. It's time to establish a different career track for people in leadership positions who don't have the "generativity"[1] reflex to be a people leader. We need titles like executive problem solver, deal maker, corporate spokesperson, business strategist, and decision maker. Perhaps being offered some such title will cue top-of-the-hierarchy people to focus on the roles and function they currently neglect. Someone needs to worry about the professional development and career progression of the employees while the salespeople are out selling. No wonder Mel missed seeing that his orientation was competitive. He lacked role models for managing.

---

[1]What Erik Erikson cites as a mature stage of an individual's ontology in *Identity and the Life Cycle* (New York: Norton, 1994).

REFERENCE POINT 5:
What Does It Take for the "Top Team" to Function Like a Team?

Recently a member of the top executive team in a company to which we were consulting handed us what he saw as an old but telling *Harvard Business Review* article.[2] That article described the difficulty company presidents have in getting direct reports to supercede the success of their work unit with company-level priorities. For example, a VP for sales typically behaves as if no other contribution counts if his or her numbers fail to progress as expected. The VP for manufacturing knows that no other contribution will matter if he or she fails to keep production up and costs down. Et cetera. But supposedly top-team meetings are forums where concern for the well-being of the company as a whole are supposed to supercede advocacy of jurisdictional interests. Cutting to the quick, the article laments the folly of such reasoning, referencing the failures such ideologically pure-of-heart top-team management groups have met.

Reflecting on the article, we thought, "That's our experience. Exactly!" Rerunning the tapes, we readily recalled a stream of occasions where we watched company leaders come up dry in getting department heads to table local unit concerns, put on their company-wide hats, and elevate their perspectives. In every instance we could see people playing the game, going through the motions, pretending to sacrifice for the overall company good and demonstrating statesmanlike gung-ho thinking. But when we looked beyond what people said to carefully observe the actions they took and what they didn't say, their verbalized commitments were seldom reified by action. We don't remember hearing a department head say, "You can reduce our budget because other areas need the money more." Nor have we heard any executive acknowledge, "I can see how our unit's actions continue to interfere with

---

[2]Jon R. Katzenbach, "The Myth of the Top Management Team," *Harvard Business Review* (November–December 1997).

other operations, and we'll make immediate changes." Neither have we found any individual believing that, when bonuses are given out, the boss will reward his or her "for the greater good" sacrifices that caused projected year-end numbers to fall short or budget to be exceeded. No, despite all the spoken words, department heads and work unit leaders have learned to get to their boss's agendas only after making sure their own agendas were served. But would they have operated differently if their "loyalty pledges" were carried out in front of the boss's boss?

Our answer to whether there would be more authentic sacrifice and greater-good thinking in response to the big boss than in response to one's direct boss is uncertain, for interpersonal chemistry and trust are always important considerations. All things being equal, percentage-wise we've seen significantly more responsiveness to higher level bosses, but we haven't kept statistics. Minimally, we contend, you won't see greater "CYA"[3] responsiveness than you're seeing right now.

REFERENCE POINT 6:
How Come the Boss Gets a Raise When His or Her Subordinates Screw Up?

Years ago a group of us had the theme and title for what we were convinced would become a best-selling business book. Just telling people the title made them want a copy. We saw it as a great-selling Christmas present and, in paperback, a show-stopper stocking stuffer. We planned on calling it "The Assholes Are Winning."

Writing it would be a breeze. All we needed were some interesting people to interview, Studs Terkel–style. For a while we conducted test interviews and immediately discovered that, on this topic, almost everyone had an interesting tale to tell. But eliciting those tales turned up so much negativity that we got depressed to the point we had to quit. As suspected, there's a great deal of per-

---

[3]The acronym *CYA* is business world jargon for "cover your anatomy."

ceived injustice in "management land," with bosses frequently seen as the villains. In many instances the charge was the boss stealing credit for what the subordinate accomplished. In many others it was the subordinate being blamed for debacles the boss had initiated and failed to brief sufficiently. Throughout there was a feeling that when it came to boss/subordinate teamwork, words of support and in-it-together guidance did not materialize in action.

Since many of our informants were also bosses and in some instances "featured players" in one of their subordinate's tales, we got to wondering, "Is there anything about an organization chart that aids and abets what people experience as negatives beyond the character flaws of the people they are describing?" In instances in which the organization chart appeared to be an amplifying influence, we found charts rampant with confusion. There were vaguely defined responsibilities with duplicating titles lying in multiple jurisdictions that caused people to fight over authorities they thought were theirs. There were people with technical know-how not asserting themselves in areas of their expertise out of fear of making someone with a higher rank feel anxious or insecure. There were people with harbored resentments intentionally withholding information for purposes of wanting to bury an individual who, on the chart, was in their way. And in every case, the storyteller's tale included his or her own retaliatory cheating and self-justified mean-spiritedness.

CONNECTING THE LAST
THREE REFERENCE POINTS

Reference points 4 through 6 are relatively easy to summarize and, added to the first three, convincingly argue that the system needs major changing. Point four shows how seasoned professionals need bosses who stage for their problem-solving success, not bosses who meddle in their assignments, cherry-pick their problems, and compete with them for glory. Instead of micromanagement by bosses performing no-fail oversight, they want macromanagement by bosses dedicated to helping them succeed. Point 5 identifies the reward and blame dilemmas that inhibit individuals from buying into higher order, comprehensive pictures of what their company needs. Point 6 characterizes the resentment subordinates hold for bosses who preach "we're in it together" but pass the buck when it comes time for a hit. Taken together these points indicate the presence of competitive forces lurking within boss/subordinate relationships that render subordinates vulnerable to the point where they spend unproductive work time watching their rear-view mirrors at the very moments they should be scanning the road ahead. These issues and the issues discussed in points 1 to 3 are what our proposal seeks to correct.

OUR BACK-POCKET PROPOSAL FEATURES TWO-STEP-UP EVALUATION

Building upon these reference points, here's our plan for changing the structure to get rid of hierarchical relationships. First, *clean up the chart*; then *kill the bosses*. Cleaning up the chart entails clarifying responsibilities, streamlining authorities, and making sure that every unit's box includes the name of an individual who actually manages. Killing the bosses entails reassigning all "green sheet," performance review authorities up one level past an individual's direct boss to the person we've been calling the big boss. This is where decisions bearing on job assignment, pay, and career progression should be made. The objective is to infuse the boss/subordinate relationship with two-sided accountability. Once the direct boss catches on, the political dynamic will change from the pursuit of self-interests to **win-win-wins** and make a two-sides-accountable, not one-sided hierarchical relationship, the relationship of choice.

This format shifts the core direct-boss function from one-sided accountability "evaluator" to two-sided accountability "stager for success." The emphasis is on supporting, guiding, coaching, and singing the subordinate's praises, not on issuing directives or engaging in any other version of false objectivity, command-and-control management.

Using this new format, the big boss evaluates large numbers of two-level down subordinates, an assignment he or she can only accomplish by relying on the direct boss's preliminary assessment and wherever possible staying macro. But big bosses will also have the subordinate's self-characterization and self-appraisal to use for cross-checking, which efficiently puts the focus on discrepancies and exceptions. Questioning an assessment will involve more than just rescrutinizing the subordinate's outputs and efforts. It should also prompt a critique of the support and coaching that person receives from the direct boss, which makes the accountability in that relationship two-sided. What's more, it will focus the big boss on what ought to be his or her primary two-sided accountability concern, the quality of the performance-enhancing relationships his or her direct reports have established with their subordinates. In this scenario, when the subordinate succeeds, all parties win. Conversely, everyone ought to be learning from a subordinate setback or a performance deficiency that doesn't improve.

Two-step-up evaluation provides another level of two-sided accountability when the aggregate of all evaluations rendered within a work unit is compared with the aggregate achievements and accomplishments of that work unit. Units that have all performers ranked positively but that fail to produce results will evoke scrutiny. Bosses who formerly were using subordinates as scapegoats to explain away negative unit results will have more difficulty distancing themselves from the blame. Personnel selection, training, and guidance in deploying subordinates for success will receive more direct boss emphasis. Likewise for big bosses. Patterns of direct boss ineffectiveness will emerge that can be used to focus a big boss on the coaching a direct boss requires.

Catapulting evaluative review upward to each individual's big boss changes accountabilities. A subordinate is accountable for performing competently and seeking help and advice. That person's boss is accountable for valid assessments, providing help to ensure success and open-mindedness to engage subordinate feedback. And that person's boss, the big boss, is accountable for ensuring that the boss deploys each subordinate to get the best that person can deliver.

Our proposal is aimed at freeing people from the intimidation of one-sided evaluation and accountability. Knowledge that the big boss will be hearing both sides of any important opinion clash implies two-sided accountability. It provides the subordinate a forum for countering what the direct boss alleges. Likewise, it provides the direct boss a place to go when he or she believes important perspectives are being overlooked since, in parallel fashion, the person two levels up will be conducting his or her evaluation. In any event, appealing a performance review will never be the most desirable path to take. Getting the review correctly stated on the front end will always be politically superior. As people figure this out, we expect an outbreak in two-sided accountability, nonhierarchical relationships.

We're now at the point where we begin encountering serious objections to what our proposal suggests. The most obvious one is from big bosses who don't like the workload that awaits them. "For example," someone will say, "consider a big boss who has six direct reports, each with eight subordinates. That's forty-eight performance reviews to give. No one can review forty-eight people and do it very well." We agree—no one can "microreview" that many people and do it well.

To perform forty-eight performance reviews, a big boss has to stay "macro." To avoid getting bogged down in too many time-consuming incidents, he or she must establish an oversight system that uses categories. Macromanagement entails "management by exception," a technique with built-in efficiency. It engages incidents involving alleged unfairness with an inductive logic aimed at applying what is learned from the incident at hand to gain understanding of how the system impacts various categories of people. This is precisely the type of data that big bosses with management titles should be accessing and using every day to improve the system iteratively.

Our proposal allows big bosses to rubber stamp a boss's preliminary review if the subordinate doesn't object. It provides bosses more reason than ever to make sure subordinates succeed and fewer reasons to compete with them for credit. The idea is to rely heavily on input from direct bosses who are stationed closer to the subordinate's performances and to minimize their need to be critical. The principle of honest reciprocity will be in play as people realize that **win-win-wins** are the only strategies guaranteed to produce success. Direct bosses will have reasons to check their command-and-control impulses, and subordinates will have reasons to be more forthcoming in candidly presenting what they believe. These are precisely the actions required for effective teamwork and partnering.

Following such a procedure smokes out executives who lack the time to manage. If our plan requires more time than an individual can devote, then we suspect that this individual is primarily working as an operative. In such instances we recommend substituting someone who actually has the time and inclination to manage and liberate human resources.

Our proposal challenges top executives to clean up and clarify their charts and to streamline organization structure. People need accurate and valid road maps to understand who has which responsibility and what authority, and who stands accountable for a given result. Otherwise, it's duplication, falling between the cracks, and pass-the-buck, with mixed authorities, political intrigue, corruption, and disorientation as usual.

In stating our proposal, we've intentionally left the specifics of implementation up to you. We didn't want to presuppose too much about your organization, its system, and the adjustments required to adopt the two-way accountability principle that we see so essential to business relationships. What we've done is point the way. The bottom-line goals are greater corporate-wide accountability by bosses and subordinates alike. This requires far more interrole helpfulness than will ever be possible with one-way accountability and a belief that individual learning is essential to corporate productivity. We need hierarchy to delineate and specify individual jurisdictions. We need two-sided accountability to give individuals the feeling that they can get helpful support and an open hearing for comments and feedback they would like to exchange. In short, we need redefined motives for bosses, motives that supplant having one's ego flattered and avoiding blame with the **win-win-win** motive to ensure that all people on the corporate team succeed.

9

What *Don't Kill the Bosses!* Can Do For You: Who Benefits and How?

In Chapter 1 we issued a stern warning: ***whenever hierarchical relationships flourish, the company loses out.*** By now we hope this admonition, together with our warnings against one-sided accountability, false objectivity, and win-win politics, and our enthusiastic endorsements of a proactive ***two-sided accountability*** mind-set are firmly implanted in your thinking. In this chapter we describe the uses you and your associates might make of the ***Don't Kill the Bosses!*** perspective.

Talk about chutzpah—our criticism of hierarchical relationships is an indictment of the greatest enterprise system known to humankind. We've spent an entire book arguing its ineffectiveness and explaining its corruption. For an index of your own ineffectiveness, merely count the number of hierarchical relationships in which you hold a subordinate's role, and tabulate what the inability to say things straight has cost you and your company. Now, if you've got the stomach, tabulate the items and numbers that those who report to you would list.

Because boss/subordinate interactions are the prototype of hierarchical relationships that go wrong, we've chosen ***Don't Kill the Bosses!*** as a metaphorical title. Inspired by our take-off of the bloodier manifesto by Shakespeare, "The first thing we do, let's kill all the [bosses,]"[1] we say this while advocating the importance of hierarchy. But it's hierarchical *structure* we advocate, with synapses sufficiently wide to counter the gravitational forces of hierarchical, one-sided, "you account to me" relationships. No relationship in which someone powerful is free to direct and impact important dimensions of another person's work life, without having to stand accountable for the quality of his or her direction and support, does your company any good. We favor hierarchy based on people with responsibility having the authority to exercise it, with accountability to all stakeholders and teammates, regardless of hierarchical level.

To get rid of hierarchical relationships, we've emphasized the importance of a clearly articulated organization chart, one that minimizes vagaries and redundancy. To operate to their potential, people need well-defined responsibilities and the authority to carry them out. Then, for the company to realize its potential, people need to be held accountable for results. When some operation doesn't produce, the boss in charge of that operation should acknowledge the problems and hold open-minded and thoughtful discussions both with hierarchical superiors and subordinates. Alarm bells should ring when a boss fails to realize results are straying from what's desired or when he or she notices but lacks the capacity to try an alternative course. That's the time for a bigger boss to get involved.

Holding the boss accountable should not mean threats and punishments or listening to excuses that blame people lower down. Standing accountable should entail the boss's acknowledging that an operation he or she has been entrusted to run has a problem and coming up with a plausible plan for engaging it. Thus we favor a brand of accountability in which people who fail to face up to and revise ineffective courses of action are put on notice that they need to do a better job of learning the lessons their experience has been trying to reveal. While favoring reassignment to firing, we strongly recommend the replacement of any individual who fails to scrutinize and learn open-mindedly.

---

[1]William Shakespeare, *Henry VI*, Part II, Act IV, Scene II. Actually Shakespeare used *lawyers* in his quote, not *bosses*. That might not have been such a bad idea, either.

Likewise for the care and feeding of people. Being a manager is supposed to include this. The term *management* is appropriately applied to the direction, maintenance, and leveraging of company resources, and at least some of those resources are people. When it comes to people, there's no such thing as "benign neglect." Managing people is a daily responsibility requiring personal involvement as well as structure. Just like machinery, people squeal and squeak when something goes awry. Managers need to position themselves to hear and react to noises that indicate malfunctioning. The sounds emanating from boss-dominated relationships are loud; what's it going to take to get them the required reaction?

When we ask people we see initiating hierarchical relationships what they are up to, in an effort to understand why they have gone "command-and-control," inevitably their answers place necessity over habit. Frequently we hear explanations that portray the initiator as a domino, toppling over in response to actions taken above. However, when we take time to eyeball the facts of a specific situation, as we did in the environmental cleanup case presented in Chapter 1, most control-oriented actions appear far more driven by habit than necessity. This issue was addressed in Chapter 3, where we explained that it's how people actually think about other people that causes them to acquiesce to hierarchical relationships. The ease with which people excuse themselves for failing to apply what they already know about people is precisely what we've labeled "the culprit." If it weren't for such bizarre reasoning, hierarchical relationships wouldn't exist.

This is why we place such significance on the type of two-sided accountability that ought to characterize dot-com start-ups. People in those companies are shareholders trying to maximize return on their human effort investments. They are entitled to hold bosses accountable for actions that impair their ability to perform competently and for actions required to make the company a success. Likewise for people in all companies and organizations in which being boss should be thought of as a job, not an imperial dynasty.

In stressing accountability, we're out to rid organizations of superfluous hierarchy emanating from organization charts with overlapping responsibilities, unclear authorities, and such a close nesting of titles that people seldom receive whole assignments. We want people positioned for up-front, candid interactions, motivated to assist one another in making the company a success.

We wrote this book to clarify what's wrong with hierarchy and to raise your consciousness about problems endemic to hierarchical relationships. We believe teams and companies are most likely to succeed when everyone works at full potential and that, minimally, requires candid pictures of what's going on and honest, thoughtful, give-and-take communications. To help you stage for this, we endorsed the benefits of a two-sided accountability mind-set and extensively discussed the logic and behavior required against a backdrop of hierarchical relationships as usual. We've provided sure-grip handles on salient features, in Tables C through E, with a composite of all in Table G.

We hope you find the *Don't Kill the Bosses!* perspective personally clarifying and powerful, and a resource for making your company even more effective. It should provide you a more accurate picture of the teamwork difficulties you've experienced and precisely what about your work relationships needs changing. Of course, the specific uses you make depend on your role and station.

HOW TOP-LEVEL EXECUTIVES CAN USE THE *DON'T KILL THE BOSSES!* PERSPECTIVE

This book has included many examples of top-level executives who appear defensive to the point that people who have constructive feedback to provide fear saying it straight and candidly to them. Ironically, these top-level executives hold positions of final-word authority that ought to position them to receive dissents, alternative ideas, and even personal criticisms with an open mind. The second case cited in Chapter 2, of the CEO who received an environmental award, is a classic example of the defensiveness and self-delusion that can obstruct a high-level executive's open-mindedness. On the other hand, many executives prize candid input and actively look for ways to get it. Such openness is exemplified in The Home Depot case described in Chapter 6. For executives like these, the

TABLE G CONTRASTING MIND-SETS: BOSS/SUBORDINATE RELATIONSHIPS		
	One-Side-Accountable, Hierarchical Relationships	Two-Sides-Accountable Relationships
Mind-Set About Human Nature	*False Objectivity* *Bosses and subordinates alike* place people in categories with standard expectations for all members of that category. *Bosses* underestimate the value of candid subordinate input and overestimate the comprehensiveness and accuracy of their own views. *Subordinates* grouse about differing viewpoints with the boss and are quick to attribute them to boss shortsightedness and disorientation.	*Inevitable Subjectivity* *Bosses and subordinates alike* assume each individual views events uniquely, according to his or her self-interests, ambitions, and self-perceived competencies. Both accept that personal considerations as well as functionality drive individual actions. *Bosses* actively seek the viewpoints of subordinates and attempt to learn what underlies the differing views. *Subordinates* who sense disagreement inquire about the boss's logic and open-mindedly follow up from there.
Mind-Set for Internal Politics	*Politics as Usual* *Bosses and subordinates alike* pursue their interests with jurisdictionally constrained interpretations of what the company requires and needs from them. They justify their activities on grounds that they are performing properly and benefiting the company. Personal and self-beneficial twists to their efforts are subliminal and hidden. *Bosses* are suspicious of subordinates' self-interested agendas. *Subordinates* resent the indulgence of bosses who pursue transparently self-serving interests.	*Win-Win-Win Politics* *Boss and subordinates alike* look for ways to conduct their self-interested, company-enhancing pursuits with consideration for like pursuits of those with whom they interact. *Bosses* respect the self-interested side of subordinates' work commitments, attempting to learn what they are and provide appropriate support. *Subordinates* are comfortable with their own and others' explicit self-interested pursuits if they align with company interests.
Mind-Set for Accountability	*One Side Accountable* *Bosses and subordinates alike* act with a mind-set that the boss ultimately gets his or her way. *Bosses* evaluate subordinates without a system they see ensuring fairness or candid, reciprocal critique. *Subordinates* must answer effectiveness questions thought up and raised by the boss, with negative consequences for "wrong" answers. Feeling open-endedly vulnerable, they seek "to purchase" a generous interpretation through deferential behavior.	*Two Sides Accountable* *Bosses and subordinates alike* recognize the bosses' authority to make decisions, but still act on a mind-set that each person on the "team" is answerable to the others. *Bosses* act accountably to all "teammates" who have a stake in the decisions they make, or results that they are charged with producing, regardless of hierarchical level. *Subordinates* take the initiative in requesting information and perspective on all topics that concern them. They think the boss's job includes staging for their personal effectiveness and success as well as concern for their development.

Don't Kill the Bosses! perspective can be used to reinforce their natural inclinations to get people below them to open up.

In any event, regardless of defensiveness and limitations in learning from one's critics, top-level executives are well positioned to facilitate and support candor in the ranks. Instituting two-level-up evaluation procedures, such as organizationally appropriate variations of the *Don't Kill the Bosses!* model described in Chapter 8, can provide a formidable beginning. It's a method for positioning bosses below them at every organizational level to see events through the eyes of the people they are supposed to help and to learn specifically what those individuals need to perform more competently and succeed. With an emphasis on two-sided accountability, they should see this perspective facilitating teamwork, which almost always is prized as the most valuable of company assets.

Pushing out further, executives implementing two-step-up evaluation will quickly discover that, serendipitously, they have initiated an extremely powerful leadership development program. Insisting that bosses stand accountable for their subordinates' performances instills a motivation for bosses at all levels to listen, learn, and reflect on why they themselves have thought differently. It creates the need to inquire as to how subordinates see events and how they see their actions accruing to produce organizationally significant results. It pushes bosses to consider alternative ways of operating, given the human resources at hand, and provides a motive for them to work on their consultative and advice-giving skills.

HOW EXECUTIVES CAN BENEFIT

By "executives," we mean individuals who lead large work units including department and division heads. By and large they have risen through the managerial ranks and are well schooled in organization politics and the "efficiencies" of one-sided, command-and-control accountability. They are proficient in the art of making self-interested opinions appear team focused and in refraining from making statements that could cause a bigger boss or associate to interpret their comments critically. In essence we're reinforcing the fifth reference point made in Chapter 8 about the skillful ways in which executives avoid making territorial concessions in power, authority, and resources, in team meetings called to optimize the functioning of the organization as a whole.

For executives, hierarchical relationships are "conveniences" that allow them to avoid repetitive and administrative managerial duties. They are indulgences that provide the opportunity to "cherry-pick," assuming a central role in those high-visibility projects they personally find most interesting. It allows them to self-promote and to justify their effectiveness in terms of actions taken instead of delivered results. On the other hand, hierarchical relationships can make their lives political nightmares. Reports who find themselves deprived of opportunity and fear lack of support, and peers whose territorial interests cause them to view events competitively, engage them in stress-producing, clandestine survival dynamics. Daily, executives find themselves watching their backsides, involved in time-consuming, just-in-case activities.

The *Don't Kill the Bosses!* perspective serves as a wake-up call for executives to join the organizational team. It directs them to stage for the effective functioning of the people reporting to them, which we call "managing." This requires learning about specific individuals and the resources, skills, and authorities they need to succeed. It redefines executive leadership to emphasize resource procurement, sounding-board reacting, and people development, with oversight an enabling process not usurping responsibility and authority. It proposes the two-sided accountability mind-set as the guideline logic in building trusting relationships. It directs executives to involve company operatives in discussions held on strategic topics germane to the work they are performing. Alternatively, it directs those who want to emphasize their roles and stewardship in corporate and domain problem solving to get out of the managerial line.

WHAT MIDDLE-LEVEL BOSSES HAVE TO GAIN

Middle-level bosses oversee customer contact point operations and are charged with implementing plans created by someone in the

hierarchy above them. Maintaining close contact with people reporting to them, they act to promote teamwork and camaraderie.
They would like to minimize hierarchical relationships and the unfairness, corruption, and self-delusion that accompany them.
However, these good intentions place them in a squeeze. Typically
their bosses expect command-and-control.

Thus we see this group as the most vulnerable organizational
echelon. What their bosses expect limits their ability to bond with
people who report to them, which is precisely what they believe
the company needs done most. Quickly they learn their personal
progress depends on lining up with their boss who appears to want
the types of results that can only be gotten with command and
control. Functioning with little idea of how to manage such dilemmas, they resort to pass-the-buck reasoning. Acknowledging unfairness about what's required, such as applying a salary curve to a
group of individuals when they allege each to be top-notch con-
tributors, they plead helplessness. They blame their boss and the
system for what they consent to do.

The *Don't Kill the Bosses!* perspective provides middle-level
bosses a logic for comprehending what's troubling them and understanding what about their own relationships and the system as a
whole needs to change. It alerts them to the dangers of making
one-sided accountability the default setting in their relationships
with subordinates and to the importance of initiating two-sides-
accountable partnerships with superiors when possible. For example, we know a middle manager who asked his boss whether he
could attend a meeting where the boss was going to brief high-
level executives on a report the manager alone had prepared. His
boss responded, "Outsiders aren't usually allowed, but since it's
your report being discussed, I can't think of a reason to turn you
down. Why don't you accompany me to the meeting, and let's see
if anyone insists that you leave." Not wanting to put himself in a
loss-of-face situation and equipped with the *Don't Kill the Bosses!*
perspective, this manager sought to hold his boss accountable. He
replied, "I prefer that you tell the group that *you* want me there
and that you think it's appropriate that I attend. Then, if you get
their agreement, call me and I'll come right over."

WHAT PEOPLE STARTING OUT AND LOWER DOWN IN THE COMPANY HAVE TO GAIN

When we think about people lower down in the organization and those just starting out, we think about the people we encounter in The Anderson School's highly regarded MBA program for the fully employed. Our model student has just turned thirty, is career-ambitious, has been working in a professional discipline for five or more years, is either a first-level manager or project supervisor, is dissatisfied either with his or her current job or the prospects of a linear progression career in the company, and plans to use his or her MBA degree as a ticket for switching jobs, disciplines, or companies. Of course, each person is different, and imputing any or all of these characteristics to a specific student will produce imprecision to the point that it doesn't apply.

Asking these students how they use their exposure to *Don't Kill the Bosses!* thinking, we find them clarifying what about their current job bothers them and what's required for an improved situation. Some have personalized their dissatisfaction with an incompetent, disinterested, or overly competitive boss, as if the problems will go away with reassignment. Some have attributed their dissatisfaction to corporate mismanagement led by a dysfunctional executive team that isn't able to ferret out incompetent performers or provide truly talented people the authority to apply their exceptional thinking. Some had thought their problems could only dissipate by switching companies. Some had seen their dissatisfaction endemic to working in a large company without share-the-wealth opportunities. Some believed the escape route lay in ground-floor participation in a new venture start-up or starting an entrepreneurial venture of their own.

In each of these situations students report that the *Don't Kill the Bosses! perspective* provides a better set of criteria for knowing what to look for in a job and what constitutes a management structure that will allow them to express themselves and succeed. People switching jobs can use the *Don't Kill the Bosses!* perspective to assert themselves in interviews, in testing for and establishing that they expect two-sided accountability relatedness. One fully employed student put it quite vividly when she said, "Finally I know what my last supervisor meant when she warned me not to date a poet." She went on to describe the teamwork and interpersonal-style questions she now brings to job interviews, a dramatic change from the way she used to be taken in by sweet talk.

CONCLUSION

We close by recognizing that the ***Don't Kill the Bosses!*** perspective represents an open-ended experiment that has yet to be fully explored. People are writing new chapters every day; perhaps you'll be one of the authors. This perspective proceeds from acknowledging that all hierarchical relationships are problematic. And it doesn't make any difference whether we're talking about corporate management, international relations, family dynamics, recreation, or sports. Hierarchical relationships corrupt.[2] No one likes being a one-sided accountability recipient, and few escape without dysfunction and negative consequence.

We're not expecting two-sided accountability to be the panacea solution for all boss/subordinate problems. Alleging this was never our intent. Our goal was to clarify a set of dilemmas that all of us have denied and avoided and to give you our best advice for coping with them. We wanted to enlist you as another field investigator searching for ways to partner with people you've been dominating and deluding, always because it seemed necessary. Now that you know better, you owe it to yourself, the people you work with, and your company to be steadfast in seeking out and building ***straight-talk communication, aboveboard politics, authentic teamwork, esprit de corps***, and ***stand-and-be-counted accountability*** relationships.

---

[2]Recall Lord Acton's warning: "Power tends to corrupt; absolute power corrupts absolutely."

Index

About the Authors

Samuel A. Culbert has developed a blunt yet sensitive way of framing situations so that all forces driving people's opinions and actions, including the subjective, self-interested, and political, can be matter-of-factly considered and explicitly discussed. Throughout his career he has creatively welded three activities: consulting, teaching, and writing. Consulting is where he encounters work effectiveness problems in their contemporary forms, learns how they are being dealt with, and finds challenge in coming up with new ways of engaging them. Teaching provides forums for extrapolating from problems to issues and, through give-and-take interaction, for probing underlying dynamics to identify which assumptions and resulting practices need upgrading. Writing is where he brings it all together to package his understanding for public consumption.

For more than twenty-five years Dr. Culbert's base of operations has been UCLA's Anderson Graduate School of Management, where he is a professor of management. Prior to assuming his UCLA post he was program director for organization studies at The NTL Institute of Applied Behavioral Sciences and an adjunct professor at The George Washington University. Dr. Culbert holds a B.S. degree in industrial engineering from Northwestern University and a Ph.D. in clinical psychology from UCLA.

Dr. Culbert has achieved wide-scale recognition as an expert and theoretician in the management field. He holds a McKinsey Award for an article published in the *Harvard Business Review* and has contributed chapters in many leading management-related books. His own books include *The Organization Trap* (Basic Books, 1974) and *The Invisible War: Pursuing Self-Interests at Work* (written with John J. McDonough; Wiley, 1980), which in 1980 won the AAP award as the best business and management book published that year. *Radical Management: Power, Politics, and the Pursuit of Trust* (also with John J. McDonough; Free Press, 1985) has just been reprinted, and *Mind-Set Management: The Heart of Leadership* (Oxford University Press, 1996) continues to garner high acclaim across the general trade market.

Dr. Culbert's consulting has specialized in executive communication and teamwork, trust building and organizational effectiveness, and leadership development and corporate strategizing. He believes consulting provides him the practical experiences and insight that enable him to teach, write, and speak with realism and clarity. Reluctant to list his clients publicly, they include a diverse representation of the private and public sectors: small companies and members of Fortune's 500; international, federal, state, and local agencies; and privately funded not-for-profit organizations. He also has extensive overseas consulting and teaching experience. A much sought-after public speaker, Dr. Culbert's respected and unconventional perspectives on contemporary management happenings have been cited in major newspapers worldwide.

John Ullmen is currently a senior manager for organizational effectiveness at Earthlink. He is in the dissertation process of a Ph.D. in management at UCLA with a study that focuses on cofounder relationships in entrepreneurial firms. Ullmen has broad independent consulting experience in teambuilding, management coaching, network analysis, organizational change, and business development. He has been a consultant in the Management Communication Program at UCLA's Anderson School of Management for the last four years and a consultant for several Internet start-up businesses. He holds a B.S. degree in engineering mechanics from the Air Force Academy and an M.S. degree in public policy from Harvard University.

Prior to becoming a consultant, John was a U.S. Air Force officer, separating as a major in the U.S. Air Force Reserve. He has worked as a lead systems engineer for the development, production, and operations of a Joint Chiefs of Staff intelligence program. For three years, he was an instructor and founding team member of the Center for Character Development at the U.S. Air Force Academy, where he trained students, faculty, and staff in character development, team building, organizational development, and personal growth.

Berrett-Koehler Publishers

BERRETT-KOEHLER is an independent publisher of books, periodicals, and other publications at the leading edge of new thinking and innovative practice on work, business, management, leadership, stewardship, career development, human resources, entrepreneurship, and global sustainability.

Since the company's founding in 1992, we have been committed to supporting the movement toward a more enlightened world of work by publishing books, periodicals, and other publications that help us to integrate our values with our work and work lives, and to create more humane and effective organizations.

We have chosen to focus on the areas of work, business, and organizations, because these are central elements in many people's lives today. Furthermore, the work world is going through tumultuous changes, from the decline of job security to the rise of new structures for organizing people and work. We believe that change is needed at all levels—individual, organizational, community, and global—and our publications address each of these levels.

We seek to create new lenses for understanding organizations, to legitimize topics that people care deeply about but that current business orthodoxy censors or considers secondary to bottom-line concerns, and to uncover new meaning, means, and ends for our work and work lives.

See next page for other publications from Berrett-Koehler Publishers

The New SuperLeadership

Leading Others to Lead Themselves

Charles C. Manz and Henry P. Sims, Jr.

"SuperLeadership" describes a style of leadership that focuses on "leading others to lead themselves." Based on the same concepts as the authors' previous bestselling book, this new edition is thoroughly revised throughout and emphasizes a pragmatic, how-to approach. It provides practical guidance for implementing Super-Leadership and features contemporary examples and profiles, many from the high-tech and knowledge-based business sectors.

Hardcover, 280 pages • ISBN: 1-57675-105-8 CIP
Item #51058-374 $27.95

The Knowledge Engine

How to Create Fast Cycles of Knowledge-to-Performance and Performance-to-Knowledge

Lloyd Baird and John C. Henderson

Baird and Henderson show how to produce knowledge as part of the work process and apply that learning to performance to create a "knowledge engine" that drives ongoing performance improvement. Built on five years of research and application in leading corporations, this book details a five-step knowledge-performance cycle.

Hardcover, 200 pages • ISBN 1-57675-104-X CIP
Item #5104X-374 $27.95

Stewardship

Choosing Service Over Self-Interest

Peter Block

Peter Block shows how to recreate our workplaces by replacing self-interest, dependency, and control with service, responsibility, and partnership. He demonstrates how a far-reaching redistribution of power, privilege, and wealth will radically change all areas of organizational governance, and shows why this is our best hope to enable democracy to thrive, our spiritual and ethical values to be lived out, and economic success to be sustained.

Paperback, 288 pages • ISBN 1-881052-86-9 CIP
Item #52869-374 $16.95

Hardcover, 7/93 • ISBN 1-881052-28-1 CIP • Item #52281-374 $24.95

Audiotape, 2 cassettes • ISBN 1-57453-147-6
Item #31476-374 $17.95

Berrett-Koehler Publishers
PO Box 565, Williston, VT 05495-9900
Call toll-free! **800-929-2929** 7 am-12 midnight
Or fax your order to 802-864-7627
For fastest service order online: **www.bkconnection.com**

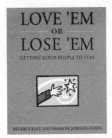

Love 'Em or Lose 'Em
Getting Good People to Stay

Beverly Kaye and Sharon Jordan-Evans

It happens time and time again: the brightest and most talented people leave the company for "better opportunities." Their peers wonder how management could let them go. Their managers feel helpless to make them stay. Beverly Kaye and Sharon Jordan-Evans explore the truth behind the dissatisfactions of many of today's workers and offer 26 strategies—from A to Z—that managers can use to address their concerns and keep them on the team.

Paperback original, 244 pages • ISBN 1-57675-073-6 CIP
Item #50736-374 $17.95

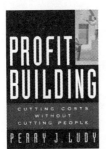

Profit Building
Cutting Costs Without Cutting People

Perry Ludy

Cultivating a loyal, productive workforce is crucial to business success. In *Profit Building,* Perry Ludy—who has worked for top companies in every major field from manufacturing to retail—introduces a five-step process called the PBP (Profit Building Process), which offers specific techniques for improving profitability by stimulating creative thinking and motivating teams to work together more effectively.

Hardcover, 200 pages • ISBN 1-57675-108-2 CIP
Item #51082-374 $27.95

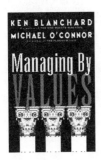

Managing By Values

Ken Blanchard and Michael O'Connor

Based on over twenty-five years of research and application, *Managing By Values* provides a practical game plan for defining, clarifying, and communicating an organization's values and ensuring that its practices are in line with those values throughout the organization.

Hardcover, 140 pages • ISBN 1-57675-007-8 CIP
Item #50078-374 $20.00

Audiotape, 2 cassettes/3 hrs. • ISBN 1-57453-146-8
Item #31468-374 $17.95

Berrett-Koehler Publishers
PO Box 565, Williston, VT 05495-9900
Call toll-free! **800-929-2929** 7 am-12 midnight

Or fax your order to 802-864-7627
For fastest service order online: **www.bkconnection.com**